Risky Business

*The Personal and Financial Costs of Small
Business Failure*

Claire Whyley

POLICY STUDIES INSTITUTE

UNIVERSITY OF WESTMINSTER

PSI is a wholly owned subsidiary of the University of Westminster

© Policy Studies Institute 1998

A CIP catalogue record of this book is available from the British Library.

ISBN 0 85374 713 X
PSI Report No. 838

Typeset by PCS Mapping & DTP, Newcastle upon Tyne
Printed by Athenæum Press Ltd, Gateshead, Tyne & Wear

Policy Studies Institute is one of Europe's leading research organisations undertaking studies of economic, industrial and social policy and the workings of political institutions. The Institute is a registered charity and is not associated with any political party, pressure group or commercial interest.

For further information contact
Policy Studies Institute, 100 Park Village East, London NW1 3SR
Tel: 0171 468 0468 Fax: 0171 388 0914 Email: pubs@psi.org.uk

Contents

Acknowledgements

This research could not have been completed without the help of a great many people, both within and outside Policy Studies Institue (PSI).

First, I would like to thank the Leverhulme Foundation for supporting the research. At PSI, I would like to thank Elaine Kempson who identified the need for research, designed the project and was successful in raising the funding for it to take place. She offered advice and support throughout the project and her input to the final report has been invaluable. I am extremely grateful for all of her hard work in getting this project to completion. I would also like to thank Claire Callender for her input to the early stages of the research, including the sampling, design of the research instruments and the fieldwork. In addition, Sue Johnson worked extremely hard to identify and track down the literature on small businesses and self-employment, and Sian Putnam's administrative assistance ensured that both the research and the production of the report ran smoothly.

The success of the fieldwork is a tribute to the hard work of many organisations and individuals. I offer sincere thanks to both Business Debtline and the Small Traders Advice Centre and Support (STACS) for their interest, enthusiasm and co-operation throughout the research. The tireless efforts, skill and commitment of our three depth interviewers – Marie Kennedy, Barbara Tilson and Chris Jacobs – produced a rich source of information on an extremely sensitive topic. Without them we would still not fully understand the impact of small business failure. Our transcribers Pat Hedges and Christina Ball also worked exceedingly hard to produce complete and accurate transcripts of, sometimes, very long and emotional interviews.

Finally, the research could not have been conducted without the willing co-operation of 40 couples/individuals who were prepared to talk to our interviewers about what was often the worst thing which had ever happened to them. I cannot thank them enough for sharing their experiences with us and helping us to understand them.

Claire Whyley was previously Research Fellow at the Policy Studies Institute. Her previous publications include *Paying for Peace of Mind: Access to home contents insurance for low-income households*. She is now a Research Fellow in the Personal Finances Research Centre at the University of Bristol.

Introduction

Small Businesses and Self-employment: the Context for Research

The years 1981 to 1991 have been viewed by many commentators as the decade in which the 'Enterprise Culture' became firmly established as a central feature of British economic policy (Storey and Strange, 1992; Keeble, Walker and Robson, 1993). One commentator remarked:

> Small firms have enjoyed a renaissance in Britain. The popular reaction against over-powerful large corporations in the 1960s and 1970s... gave way to the 'enterprise culture' of the Thatcher years... They have provided job opportunities at a time when larger companies have continued to retrench, and have often been the only source of new jobs in unemployment blackspots. Small firms, above all, are regarded as embodying a dynamism and willingness to take risks that has given a new verve to the British economy. (ESRC, undated)

From the early 1980s, small businesses were a growing phenomenon in the British economy after 'almost thirty years of continuous decline' (ESRC, undated). Political, economic and research interest in small businesses focused, in particular, on the increasing importance of this form of employment within the labour market. For many years, the small firm sector of the economy was viewed by the Conservative government as the definitive answer to employment creation and wealth generation (Johnson, 1986).

Not only were the 1980s a 'renaissance period' for small firms, they also signalled fundamental changes in the type and nature of people who were entering this sector of employment activity (Storey and Strange, 1992; Johnson, 1986; Hakim, 1989; Carter and Cannon, 1988; Brown, 1994). The profile of the self-employed population, in particular, became sufficiently altered for a clear distinction to be made between the 'new' and the existing self-employed (Meagher et al, 1994). Over-represented among the new self-employed were women; young people; people entering self-employment from unemployment or economic inactivity; part-time workers; and people past retirement age (Campbell and Daly, 1992; Meagher et al, 1994).

SMALL BUSINESS FAILURE

While the growth of the small business sector was viewed with optimism among political and economic commentators, others, advice workers and debt counsellors in particular, were expressing concern.

As small businesses and self-employment continued to grow during the 1980s and early 1990s, the number of business failures also began to grow alongside. The UK may have had the highest levels of inflows into self-employment during the 1980s, but the 'dynamic' nature of self-employment in Britain was characterised by similarly high outflows (Meagher et al, 1994). High rates of insolvency and business failure among small firms led to doubts about the extent to which this form of employment offered a long-term solution to economic problems (Thwaites and Wynarczyk, 1993). As one commentator remarked,

> ...recent record insolvencies, personal bankruptcies and business failures, coupled with rapidly increasing unemployment and a significant decrease in VAT registrations, has taken the shine off the 1980s small business 'miracle'. (Gray, 1992, p.59).

Firms are most vulnerable in the first few years of trading (DTI, 1994) and around 40 per cent of new businesses cease to trade within three years of start-up (Storey, Watson and Wyncarczyk, 1989). The vulnerability of new business ventures was illustrated by the fact that Keeble, Walker and Robson (1993) found creation rates of small businesses to be the dominant factor in rates of closure. The implications of these findings are particularly important in the context of the huge increase in the numbers of small business registrations during the 1980s.

Specialist advisors working with sole traders and small enterprises find it difficult to locate comprehensive figures available to show the true extent of small business failure. The best figures that are currently available are VAT registrations and deregistrations which provide a reasonably good starting point, although they exclude businesses operating below the VAT registration threshold. On average, around 11 per cent of businesses deregister each year. Until 1990 the rate of deregistration of small businesses was increasing at much the same rate as small business stocks (DTI, 1994). Yet between 1990 and 1996 statistics from the Department of Trade and Industry, shown in Table I.1, indicate that deregistrations increased at a faster rate than the registration of new firms (DTI, 1997).

In fact, 1996 was the first year since 1990 that new registrations outnumbered deregistrations. This revival has continued and in the first quarter of 1997 business start-ups reached their highest levels since 1989 (Barclays, 1997).

Table I.1 – *VAT registrations and deregistrations in the UK, 1980–96*[1,2]

| Year | Numbers | | | | Percentages | |
	Initial stock	Registering	Deregistering	Net change	Registering	Deregistering
1980	1,304,390	160,549	145,268	15,281	12	11
1981	1,319,671	154,135	122,592	31,543	12	9
1982	1,351,214	168,278	148,316	19,962	12	11
1983	1,371,176	182,552	148,080	34,472	13	11
1984	1,405,648	184,573	155,087	29,486	13	11
1985	1,435,134	184,866	166,758	18,108	13	12
1986	1,453,242	193,754	169,068	24,686	13	12
1987	1,477,928	211,793	172,581	39,212	14	12
1988	1,517,140	245,802	179,651	66,151	16	12
1989	1,583,291	258,838	181,005	77,833	16	11
1990	1,661,124	239,107	191,838	47,269	14	12
1991	1,708,393,	204,564	209,844	−5,280	12	12
1992	1,628,000	187,000	226,000	−39,000	11	14
1993	1,589,000	191,000	213,000	−22,000	12	13
1994[3]	1,629,235	168,240	188,140	−19,900	10	12
1995[4]	1,609,335	163,960	173,230	−9,270	10	11
1996	1,600,065	168,200	156,965	11,2335	11	10

Source: Department of Trade and Industry (1997).

1 Large increases in the threshold in 1991 and 1993 mean that estimates for 1980–1991 are not directly comparable.

2 Figures for 1980–93 count VAT reporting units. Figures for 1994–96 count whole VAT registered enterprises.

3 Excludes around 5,000 deregistrations thought to have been caused by the large rise in the turnover threshold for registration in November 1993.

4 Excludes around 4,000 deregistrations thought to have been caused by the change in the VAT partial exemption rules in 1995.

In 1992, when the number of deregistrations was highest, they accounted for 14 per cent of business stock (Campbell and Daly, 1992). During this period, more than 200,000 businesses were closed. Deregistrations do not always indicate small business failure: they may also reflect other factors such as old age, ill health or a chosen move back into employee status. However, it is safe to say that during the late 1980s and early 1990s, many thousands of people experienced small business failure.

ISSUES FOR RESEARCH

Although small business failure has generated research interest in recent years, attention has focused primarily on the numbers of businesses involved rather than on its impact on the individuals concerned. Yet a range of research projects conducted by PSI during the early 1990s identified business failure as a major contributory factor in debt and financial insecurity. This research, coupled with evidence provided by specialist advice agencies set up to deal with problems associated with business debt, identified a number of research issues relating to the lives and financial circumstances of people experiencing business failure.

First, the risk of financial difficulties for people who had set up small businesses increased quite dramatically during the 1990s. A major national study of credit and debt (Berthoud and Kempson, 1989) found relatively low levels of debt among this group. Yet by 1993/94, a study of credit card default indicated self-employed people as one of the high risk groups (Rowlingson and Kempson, 1994). The most commonly cited reason for financial difficulty among this group was business problems and mortgage arrears. In fact, in a study of mortgage arrears and possessions, almost a quarter of people with mortgage arrears and a third of those whose homes had been repossessed had suffered a loss of income due to business failure. Further, 18 per cent of possessions cases and 12 per cent of people in arrears cited business failure as the *main* reason why they had been unable to pay their mortgage (Ford et al, 1995).

Second, specialist advice agencies working with small businesses noted the high proportion of personal, as well as business, debts resulting from small business failure (Birmingham Settlement, 1991). Storey and Strange (1992) found that personal finances were the main source of funding a small business start-up. Anecdotal evidence from debt counsellors also suggested that people running small businesses did not make a clear distinction between business and personal finances. Consequently, they were particularly vulnerable to high levels of personal liability should their business encounter problems, as financial difficulties in the business sphere quickly spilled over into the personal. Further, where personal wealth and assets are used as security for business loans, small business failure can result in huge personal losses as well as the loss of the business. For example, a study by Birmingham Settlement (1991) found that small business failure almost always threatened the family home where business loans had been secured upon it.

Third, people who have run up debts as a result of small business failure often encounter serious difficulties in obtaining appropriate and affordable advice as there is very little professional support for people in this position. Most cannot afford the services of an accountant or insolvency practitioner.

Further, they frequently 'fall through the net' of traditional advice services. Voluntary advice agencies such as the Citizen's Advice Bureaux are not licensed to advise on business debts unless the business has officially ceased to trade. In addition, debts resulting from small business failure are usually far in excess of 'typical' consumer debt and, because of the mix of commercial and consumer creditors, can be extremely complicated to unpick. Finally, people who have experienced small business failure frequently require a more 'holistic' advice service than traditional debt counselling services can provide. People whose businesses have failed often suffer from a range of problems in addition to debt, including loss of physical and psychological well-being, relationship breakdown and, often, homelessness.

In fact, two specialist advice agencies, dealing specifically with issues relating to small businesses, were launched in the early 1990s. Both organisations were set up to fill the gap in traditional advice services and tackle a whole range of financial and personal problems associated with small business failure. This research was supported and informed by these two agencies.

AIMS AND OBJECTIVES OF THE RESEARCH

The main aim of this research on the personal and financial costs of small business failure was to fully explore the impact of small business failure on the lives of the people affected by it. Within this broad aim, the study focused on:

- developing an understanding of the context of small business failure, including an analysis of why people become self-employed;
- exploring the way in which self-employed people organised their business and personal finances;
- understanding the context in which business and personal debts accrue as a result of business problems;
- assessing the full financial impact of small business failure for the people involved and their families; and
- identifying the extent to which small business failure affects the physical and mental health and family relationships of people affected by it.

This report draws on the results of a depth interview survey of 40 people who had contacted a specialist advice agency about problems relating to small business failure. Around half of the sample were people whose business had failed; the remainder were still trading at the time of the research, although the majority had serious business problems and were struggling to keep afloat. Further details of the methodology used for this research are in Appendix A.

THE STRUCTURE OF THE REPORT

This report begins by exploring the routes by which people had set up a small business, identifying their reasons for doing so and the context in which their decision-making occurred. Chapter 1 introduces a typology of routes into self-employment among people whose businesses were struggling or had failed, incorporating their personal characteristics; reasons for becoming self-employed; attitudes to self-employment; and experiences of 'push' and 'pull' factors. The chapter goes on to assess the influence of routes into self-employment on the types of businesses people set up.

The second chapter looks in detail at the financial arrangements set in place by people whose businesses were struggling or had failed. It begins by assessing the nature and extent of personal investment in business start-ups, looking at variations in sources of start-up funds according to routes into self-employment and identifying the problems people faced in arranging the finance to set up a business. It also charts the nature and extent of subsequent investment into the business. Following this, the chapter explores the different ways in which people managed their business and personal finances and the extent to which they overlapped. Finally, it identifies a range of factors which are associated with a lack of separation between business and personal finance. The chapter concludes with a brief analysis of the consequences of confusing these two sources of finance.

The third chapter explores the broad context of small business failure and the circumstances in which people made the decision to close. The context in which small business failure occurred was influenced by people's routes into self-employment; their ability to cope with running a small business; the type of business they had set up; and their financial situation. The chapter also charts the emotional struggle which people encountered in making the decision to close down a small business.

The last two chapters look in detail at the impact of small business failure on the lives of the people involved. Although, in reality, the financial and personal impacts of small business failure are intricately entwined, for the purposes of this report they are identified and assessed separately. Chapter 4 looks at the financial implications of the run-up to small business failure, during which 'head in the sand' tactics frequently exacerbate both the nature and extent of financial problems. The chapter assesses the level of losses – business and personal – which result from business failure, explores decision-making around bankruptcy and its impact on people's lives. The chapter concludes by summarising the long-term financial consequences of small business failure.

The final chapter takes a wider perspective on small business failure, assessing its impact on people's physical health and psychological well-being. It also explores the way in which business failure affects people's relationships with others – both inside and outside the businesses. Finally, it assesses the impact of small business failure on spouses/partners and the wider family unit.

Chapter 1

Routes into Self-employment

The circumstances of people's decisions to become self-employed can have a crucial influence over their experiences of running a business. Routes into self-employment influenced not simply the timing and nature of people's self-employed careers but also the level of control they had over their working lives and the choices available to them when they encountered business problems. A number of different routes into self-employment were apparent even within a relatively small sample of people. They displayed quite widely different personal characteristics, family circumstances, employment histories, labour market positions and attitudes to self-employment. These factors were of key importance in influencing people's experience of being self-employed and shaping the impact of small business failure.

CHOOSING SELF-EMPLOYMENT: TRADITIONAL PERCEPTIONS

Current understanding of individuals' personal motivations for entry into self-employment is relatively unsophisticated. According to previous research, popular perceptions of the 'self-employed' are of independent, risk-taking entrepreneurial individuals who choose self-employment because they value the independence, freedom and financial returns it offers. Blanchflower and Oswald (1990) refer to these people as:

> Hardy individualists, [preferring] the flexibility and potential financial rewards of self-reliance, even if it brings greater risks. (Blanchflower and Oswald, 1990; p 133).

This type of person may, indeed, be well-represented among prominent and successful self-employed people or, even, among the majority of the self-employed population. They were far less in evidence, however, among people whose businesses were struggling or had failed.

Existing literature usually presents decision-making around self-employment as a rational process of evaluation, weighing up the advantages of self-employment in relation to its alternatives. Johnson (1986), for example, argues that:

> ...a person will move into self-employment when he perceives that the returns from such employment exceed those obtainable from the alternative uses of his time. (Johnson, 1986; p.79)

Studies of self-employment tend to agree that its attraction results from both monetary and non-monetary returns. Individuals' perceptions of these returns form a set of push and pull factors which provide the context for decision-making.

Monetary returns

It is suggested that people enter self-employment because they perceive its monetary rewards to be greater than the possible returns to be gained from employee status (Johnson, 1986). This is more attractive to individuals who feel they should be entitled to all the profits of their labour. However, financial returns from self-employment have been found to be cited less frequently as the main motivation for moving into self-employment than the non-monetary factors discussed below (Hakim, 1989; Blanchflower and Oswald, 1990; Campbell and Daly, 1992).

Non-monetary returns

Non-monetary returns from self-employment are numerous and can be both positive and negative. Positive motivations tend to centre on the psychological satisfaction gained from self-employment including independence, autonomy and the opportunity for innovation (Johnson, 1986). More negative reasons for perceiving higher returns from self-employment include frustration with employee status; an inability to progress as an employee; and a fear of unemployment or redundancy (Johnson, 1986). Women were found to be particularly likely to have entered self-employment as a result of bad experiences as employees (Carter and Cannon, 1988). In addition, the increased likelihood of self-employment among ethnic minorities and disabled people suggests that it may provide better prospects for people in 'socially marginal groups' (Johnson, 1986) who may be disadvantaged in the labour market.

Push and pull factors

The factors which have been found to influence the decision to become self-employed can be divided into push and pull factors.

Push factors occur when the anticipated returns from being an employee are reduced. The most frequently mentioned push factors are actual or threatened unemployment or redundancy; the inability to progress in large enterprises; and reduced opportunities for employees in general (Johnson, 1986; Hakim, 1989). Pull factors occur when, all other things being equal, the anticipated returns from self-employment are perceived to be higher than its alternatives. The most frequently mentioned pull factors are independence, autonomy, flexibility and financial rewards (Johnson, 1986; Hakim, 1989; Gray, 1992). Pull factors also occur when self-employment is perceived as a route out of dependence – either on contractual, paid employment or on social security benefits (Brown, 1994).

In general, it is believed that pull factors are more significant in explaining increases in self-employment than push factors (Hakim, 1989; Storey and Strange, 1992):

> Only around a quarter of the... self-employed could be classified as involuntary or, at the least, reluctant entrants to self-employment. Even within this minority, push factors were often complemented by other, more positive reasons for setting up in business.(Hakim, 1989, p.290)

Self-employed people are, in general, more likely to cite positive than negative reasons as their motivation for becoming self-employed (Hakim, 1989; Storey and Strange, 1992). Further, it appears that self-employment per se has attractions which are distinct from the desire to set up a particular type of business (Hakim, 1989).

ROUTES INTO SELF-EMPLOYMENT: A TYPOLOGY

The in-depth approach taken by this research sheds more light on the reasons why some people become self-employed and, crucially, illustrates the differential chances of success which result from different routes into self-employment. This typology clearly cannot be applied to all self-employed people, because of the particular nature of our sample. It does, however, add a key dimension to our understanding of routes into self-employment among people who experience serious business problems or whose businesses fail. In particular, it illustrates that routes into self-employment can vary widely among different groups of self-employed people and provides a better understanding of the reasons why people who do not correspond to traditional stereotypes of self-employment become self-employed. Finally, the typology highlights the importance of routes into self-employment in defining and, for some, determining the nature and success of a small business.

The research findings indicate a number of key differences between people whose businesses were struggling or had failed and traditional perceptions of the self-employed population.

- Many did not conform to the traditional '*hardy individualist*' image and did not hold the attitudes which are traditionally associated with self-employed people.
- Decision-making around self-employment was frequently not the result of a rational exercise of weighing-up the relative costs and benefits of self-employment against other types of employment status.
- A notable proportion of the people in our sample were not enticed into self-employment by pull factors. Indeed, for some it was difficult to identify any pull factors at all.

By identifying and assessing the importance of factors such as personal and family circumstances, employment history and motivations for entry into self-employment, it is possible to go beyond Meagher et al's classification of the 'new' and 'old' self-employed (Meagher et al, 1994). People whose businesses were struggling or had failed can be classified into four categories in terms of their entry into self-employment. In fact, it was possible to identify four broad routes into self-employment: *reluctant recruits, constrained choice entrants, positive choice entrants and entrepreneurs*. These are outlined in Table 1.1 and discussed in more detail below.

THE RELUCTANT RECRUITS

As Table 1.1 indicates, the reluctant recruits did not aspire to be self-employed. They expressed a strong desire to obtain work as employees but were unable to find it and felt they had been forced into self-employment by circumstances beyond their control. As a consequence, their entry into self-employment was almost entirely by default and largely for negative reasons.

Personal characteristics

The reluctant recruits were among the oldest people in the sample. Their ages at the time they started their businesses ranged from 52–60. Several expressed the view that they were 'too old to find a job' and feared that their opportunities to find work were reduced by ageism in the labour market:

Table 1.1 – *Typology of routes into self-employment*

Category	Characteristics
Reluctant recruits	• Entered self-employment with great reluctance. • Wanted to work as employees but no labour market opportunities available. • Self-employment offered the only opportunity to work. • No positive attitudes towards self-employment.
Constrained choice entrants	• Entered self-employment because of disadvantage in the labour market. • Would have preferred work as employees. • Unable to find suitable employee work due to restricted labour market opportunities. • Some positive attitudes to self-employment – believed it offered some good opportunities.
Positive choice entrants	• Chose self-employment because it offered the best opportunities at the time. • Successful employees, entered self-employment after experiencing a 'trigger' factor. • May not have considered self-employment without trigger factor. • Very positive attitudes to self-employment – enthusiastic about opportunities.
Entrepreneurs	• Perceive self-employment as the 'natural' state; always aspired to self-employment. • Unhappy and/or unable to progress as employees. • Few opportunities to do well as an employee. • Very positive attitudes to self-employment – believed it offers the best opportunities.

And the opportunities weren't there... of course, now the age thing comes into it because, as in most jobs, with selling in particular, once you get over the age of thirty-five to forty you've got no chance... And I was prepared to be a rep or anything, I wasn't looking for management or anything like that... I just needed to earn...

Their perception of age discrimination was heightened by the expectation that it would get worse as they got older. This created a pressure to act quickly.

Reluctant recruits were further disadvantaged by their educational and employment backgrounds. None of them had any formal qualifications to give them an advantage in their search for work. Neither had they built up any skills or trade experience which they could 'sell' in the labour market. Most had rather chequered employment histories, characterised by frequent movement between a range of manual, unskilled jobs often in construction or manufacturing. They also showed a particular vulnerability to redundancy and recurring episodes of unemployment. Yet despite their disadvantage in the labour market, their commitment to work was very strong. They were determined not to rely on benefits for the rest of their lives.

In addition, reluctant recruits had often been the sole wage earner in their household and desperately needed to earn enough money to support their whole family. One woman, for example, needed to earn enough money to support herself, her sick husband, her daughter and her very elderly mother who she cared for at home. Other reluctant recruits had fewer family responsibilities but were nevertheless still under a great deal of pressure to find some kind of paid work. Few had partners who were in employment, which meant that the whole financial burden for 'keeping' the household fell on them.

Reluctant recruits were all home owners and were under pressure to find a reliable way of earning the money they needed to pay their mortgages. Although they would have received mortgage interest payments while they were receiving Income Support, this was not a long-term solution. All of them were approaching retirement age and were anxious to have secure living arrangements in retirement.

Why did they become self-employed?

Three of the nine people in this category perceived themselves to have been actively coerced into self-employment, largely against their will. The first, a young Asian man, was forced to leave full-time education to run the family business. The business had previously been run by another family member who had decided to leave. A replacement had to be found from within the family or the business would have closed down. This man's decision-making was heavily influenced by cultural pressures to keep the business within the family. He explained:

> ... *my father basically approached me and said 'Look, at the end of the day either we keep this business, which is a good business or I lock it up and it all goes to waste... so the choice is yours'.*

He described his move into self-employment as '*not through choice but necessity*'.

Another person was forced into self-employment by more structural factors. She, with her husband and daughter, had managed a pub for a large brewery for some years. They were very happy as managers and although they had originally wanted a tenancy, which would have given them more autonomy, they had settled for management, having been turned down as tenants by the brewery. This situation had grown to suit them:

> *Well we wanted to be tenants from the start, years ago but we could only get management. So we did management... and then we was quite happy at that.*

However, a ruling by the Monopolies and Mergers Commission in 1991 meant that the brewery was required to sell some of its pubs. So, having been unable even to obtain a tenancy in the past, she was faced with having to buy her pub and take total responsibility for it. She faced the prospect with great reluctance but no other alternative:

> *No, I didn't see any advantages in owning it really apart from having a roof over our heads, because it was only a little village pub you know, and no matter what you did it wouldn't make enough... [and] there was the mortgage to pay.*

This reluctance was fuelled by the fact that her husband had developed a drink problem which she feared would be worse if they owned the stock, rather than simply selling it on the brewery's behalf:

> *... I felt uncomfortable with it from the beginning, because mainly of my husband's drinking as well, I thought there's no way I can make money while he's drinking all the profits.*

She described her frame of mind at the time she was making her decision about self-employment as '*worried sick*'. The fact that the pub was the family home as well as its sole source of income added to the pressure.

The last case of 'coercion' into self-employment related to a man who was nearing retirement age and who, having been unemployed for some years, was strongly advised to join the Enterprise Allowance scheme by staff at his local DS office.

> *I still went to try and find work, I was still looking for work and if I could have found more part-time work I would have... hopefully signed off... so... they said, 'Why don' t you go on the Enterprise Allowance?'... and I said, 'Well, is that a good option or not?'...and they said 'Oh yeah, definitely'.*

In fact, he had no skills or trade that he could use in a business, had suffered with poor health for some years and, crucially, was so badly dyslexic that he was registered disabled. Yet he was pressured by DS staff to move onto the Enterprise Allowance Scheme. He remarked '*I don't know if I was invited or press-ganged really*'.

Other reluctant recruits felt they had been forced into self-employment by more indirect pressures. Unable to find any other kind of paid work, self-employment offered them their only real prospect of escaping long-term unemployment. One had been unemployed for seven years, another for almost two years. Neither felt that they had any prospect of finding employment:

> *... in a period of six months I got two thousand five hundred CVs out from Toronto to Tokyo, from Zanzibar to Zambia, you know, from Antigua to Australia. I literally went round the world... couldn't get in... I started to think, 'Look, you're getting older, you're now in your late 50s'... and I thought 'what am I going to do?'*

For another respondent, self-employment offered protection against labour market insecurity. Having already experienced redundancy twice, he did not feel he could face it again. For him, self-employment was a safety net:

> *... it was something to fall back on, I'd been made redundant from ABC.... [and] DEF... and I could see the job with XYZ going under.*

All of the reluctant recruits would have preferred to do something other than set up a business. The majority wanted to work as employees, the young Asian man wanted the chance to complete his degree and pursue a career. But their circumstances pushed them into self-employment.

Attitudes to self-employment

The importance of attitudes to self-employment lies in the impact they have on people's mind-sets at the time they set up their business. Enthusiastic anticipation, confidence in the ability to do well and the perception of self-employment as the best option are all factors which are likely to predispose an individual to cope well with new situations and a new working environment. Those who, at the other extreme, view self-employment as something into which they were forced and who would prefer to be working as an employee are less likely to cope well with new experiences and change.

For the reluctant recruits, entry into self-employment was a decision over which they had little control and for which they showed very little enthusiasm. They were adamant that they had become self-employed because it was the only option available to them and that they would have made very different choices in other circumstances.

> *Don't forget I had over two thousand five hundred CVs out which only
> yielded ten interviews... so it was a very bleak business scenario.*

It was their strong commitment to work which led them to set up in
business, rather than positive attitudes towards self-employment itself.
Their primary aim was to find some kind of paid work to support their
families. Indeed, this was the only good thing one respondent could
identify about being self-employed.

> *At least I'm not a burden on the country, am I? At least I'm looking
> after myself, one way or another.*

Their level of commitment to labour market activity of some kind was
so strong that it over-rode even their considerable resistance to the idea
of self-employment.

> *It was an arrangement when I had no choice, a drowning man catches
> a straw... Instead of staying on the dole I did this business.*

Push versus pull factors

The reluctant recruits were clearly, and in their own words, pushed into
self-employment. They could identify no attractions to self-employment
per se. One was shown a list of the factors generally perceived to be
advantages of self-employment, including independence, autonomy,
freedom and so on, and asked which were relevant to her decision to
become self-employed. She was unable to apply any of these factors to
her decision-making processes saying only *'we was forced into it really.'*

The importance of self-employment was that it offered a pathway
out of their current situations. It represented an 'opportunity' only by
virtue of the fact that they were unlikely to be presented with any alternatives. In this respect, reluctant recruits' entry into self- employment
was less a decision than a practical necessity.

CONSTRAINED CHOICE ENTRANTS

In some respects, this group was similar to the reluctant recruits. The
majority of constrained choice entrants also became self-employed
because they were disadvantaged in the labour market. However, the
circumstances in which they made their decisions regarding self-employment were qualitatively different from those faced by the reluctant
recruits in terms of their attitudes to self-employment and the opportunities it offered them.

Personal characteristics

Although constrained choice entrants were slightly younger than the reluctant recruits – the majority were in their 40s or early 50s – they still felt that their age restricted their chances of finding employment:

> *I thought, 'I've got to make a living' and I was fifty-one so I thought 'Can I get a job?'... at the time, 1980, was a recession...*

However, they were less burdened by family responsibilities than the reluctant recruits and were under less pressure to provide for an extended family network or a family member with special needs. In addition, they often had partners who were in part-time paid work which meant that they could rely on some regular money coming into the household.

The most important distinction between the reluctant recruits and constrained choice entrants, however, was their labour market position. The latter group came from more stable and successful employment backgrounds than reluctant recruits. The majority had a trade or were skilled in a particular type of work which they had pursued for long stretches of their working lives. In contrast to the range of driving, construction, and manufacturing jobs which had been held by the reluctant recruits, among the constrained choice entrants were a mechanical engineer, a qualified shoe-maker, a building services engineer and a skilled carpenter.

Why did they become self-employed?

Although constrained choice entrants, like reluctant recruits, often entered self-employment from economic inactivity, this tended to be due to redundancy rather than prolonged or repeated stretches of unemployment. In addition, constrained choice entrants had not been without work for as long as the reluctant recruits.

Some had, however, experienced redundancy more than once and found it very unsettling. One, who had enjoyed a relatively stable, successful career in building services before the recession explained:

> *... when I was made redundant for a second time I felt I couldn't trust anyone...*

The experience of redundancy, particularly towards the end of a relatively stable career, was a significant blow to his confidence. He began to question his worth and security in the employment market and felt quite vulnerable.

Other constrained choice entrants were economically active at the time they decided to become self-employed but were experiencing problems in their jobs. In fact, two left employee jobs as a result of workplace bullying.

For example, an Asian man, aged 55, had arrived in the UK in his early twenties. Despite being a trained shoe-maker in Pakistan he had been unable to secure anything more than manual, unskilled work in the UK. However, he had a fairly stable employment history and was relatively happy in his work until a new foreman took over as his supervisor. From this point on the respondent was subject to continual bullying and harassment. Despite winning an industrial tribunal, things did not improve and the situation simply '*wore him down*'.

Another man had worked in the same trade for over 20 years. At the time he made his decision to become self-employed he had worked for the same firm for seven years without any problems. However, he was dismissed without warning by his employer after making a mistake and was subsequently awarded damages for unfair dismissal by an industrial tribunal.

In theory, both of these respondents could have returned to their jobs after industrial tribunals found in their favour. However, their experiences had been so damaging that they did not feel able to return.

Like the reluctant recruits, constrained choice entrants would have preferred to work as employees, but were unable to find anything suitable. One explained:

> *I was looking for mainly getting back into employment, of any sort, maybe in a similar field that I was before the redundancy... nothing was coming up.*

In addition, having had their confidence shaken by job insecurity, redundancy or harassment, they felt that they were unlikely to find suitable employment or were concerned about the stability of the jobs which were available.

Others had particular needs from paid work which they were unlikely to be able to fulfil as employees. For example, as managers of social clubs, one couple had spent a great deal of time moving around the country to take up work wherever it was available. As they became older they were keen to move nearer to their families but had little prospect of finding suitable jobs. Self-employment offered a geographical mobility that they could never have achieved as employees.

> *You see we had a good job up there, we had a nice house, it was alright... but I wanted to come back... to move back down to the Midlands... if somebody had come up and said, 'There's a [job] going*

in Newark'... we'd have gone for that, but we couldn't see anything else we could do to get back down here without taking the pub...

Another respondent who had health problems may have been unable to continue working without the flexibility offered by self-employment. He was both disabled and sick, suffering from partial blindness, heart problems and high blood pressure. While self-employment was certainly not an easy option, it relieved him of the pressures of travelling to and from a workplace, working in alien surroundings and coping with strangers at work. In self-employment, he could set up his own workshop in familiar surroundings, receive help from family members and work at his own pace.

So, while self-employment may not have been the first choice for constrained choice entrants, unlike the reluctant recruits, it was not their last. Despite preferring to be an employee, self-employment offered a range of opportunities which were not available to them elsewhere.

Attitudes to self-employment

But, like the reluctant recruits, constrained choice entrants were unlikely to have considered self-employment if other forms of employment had been available. As a result, their attitudes towards self-employment were not overwhelmingly positive, but focused, instead, on its practical advantages.

They looked forward to the independence and freedom it offered:

I just wanted to be my own boss... not answer to anybody...

I thought being employed was a secure job at the time but... you were tied down, you know...

One described it as an opportunity to spend more time at home and invest in his family. Another was very proud at the thought of having a business which *'was something I could leave for my children'*.

They also recognised that, on balance, self-employment offered higher rewards than being employed by others. One said:

I thought, 'Well, I've missed the chance', thirty years I've been there and I've seen other people make a lot of money being self-employed... and I thought, 'Well, I'll give it a try...

Another explained:

> *... you always hear people doing well in business, they're making a lot of money and that sort of thing, so we decided we might make a good living out of it...*

It is important to note, however, that they tended not to recognise these advantages until after they had accepted that self-employment was the only real opportunity available to them.

Push versus pull factors

The most accurate assessment of the role of push and pull factors in constrained choice entrants' decisions is that:

- they were pushed to consider self-employment in the first instance;
- their decision to become self-employed was more influenced by push factors given the constraints on their labour market opportunities; but
- having decided to enter self-employment, they recognised the potential pull factors and believed that they would benefit from them.

Constrained choice entrants clearly experienced more of an interplay between push and pull factors than reluctant recruits. Although they had other choices, they were still fairly restricted in the opportunities available to them. Their main concern about employee status was the lack of stability it offered them. In addition, their requirements of employment were often more complex than a need simply to secure an income. Consequently, they were more aware of the potential rewards from self-employment than reluctant recruits and did mention some of the pull factors associated with self-employment, such as flexibility, independence and a higher earning potential. This undoubtedly increased the attraction of self-employment for them, albeit somewhat 'after the fact'.

POSITIVE CHOICE ENTRANTS

Positive choice entrants displayed many of the characteristics traditionally associated with self-employment. On the whole, they were successful employees, enticed into self-employment by its potential rewards.

Personal characteristics

Positive choice entrants were younger than any other group of respondents in the study, with ages ranging from mid-twenties to early forties. Their labour market opportunities were not restricted by their age and they still had plenty of time to find their 'niche'.

They were relatively unencumbered by family responsibilities. Being younger than the other groups in the sample, they tended not to be married or, at least, not to have dependent children. The few who did have children at the time they started their business had partners who were in stable employment and could provide a secure source of income for the household.

They also had far more options available to them when they decided to enter self-employment than the people in the other three groups. Virtually all of them were trained in a skill or, frequently, a profession which gave them a wider range of options in either employment or self-employment. They had been employees long enough to build up a good level of experience and expertise which increased their worth, even in a competitive labour market. Positive choice entrants, more than any other group in the typology, were in the enviable position of being able to consider a range of employment opportunities and select the one which they believed offered the highest rewards.

Why did they become self-employed?

Most entered self-employment straight from employment because they felt that it offered better opportunities than other forms of employment.

For example, one man in his early twenties was feeling increasingly dissatisfied with his employment situation. He worked in a large, public service industry and he felt that changes to its rigid hierarchy had thwarted his prospects for progression.

> ... the cadets were taken on as like a fast track management when I started but unfortunately the year after I started the YTS came into being and so the cadet and that was scrapped... So instead of moving through the ranks quickly... I was actually left, at like eighteen or nineteen, with no sort of career path at all... I was [at] the wrong time at the wrong place.

Changes in their working environment were important factors for other positive choice entrants. Several found themselves having to adjust to changes in company philosophy and working practices at a time when they had believed themselves to be well-established in their careers.

They found this both difficult and unsettling.

> *I was working for the company for what twelve or thirteen years... and they sold to another office equipment company that took over the staff and the company... I found it very difficult to get on with the people there and they were doing things which I didn't think was the proper way... Basically they was actually conning the customer and I didn't particularly want to work like that.*

A few others had simply experienced a *ceteris paribus* increase in the attraction of self-employment in comparison with other forms of employment. This was the case for one woman in her thirties who, as an employee, had spotted a gap in the market. The knowledge that she could fill this gap made her feel very positive about self-employment. Another positive choice entrant, who had been very successful as an employee, was attracted to self-employment by the opportunity it presented to 'give something back to society' by providing jobs for other people. Others simply felt that, having gained experience as employees, self-employment offered an opportunity to provide a better service to clients and customers.

> *I knew the ins and outs, I knew what had to be done and I knew I could do a better job than the big company because they had more overheads to pay so they cut corners to make more money...*

At the time positive choice entrants were making decisions about self-employment most of them had the option to remain in their current job or to seek a new employer. Their decision to enter self-employment reflected a perception that it offered considerably better opportunities than employee status.

Few positive choice entrants had been economically inactive immediately before they became self-employed. Some had been made redundant from relatively high powered positions, offering generous redundancy packages, and they usually made the transition to self-employment very smoothly, without a period of unemployment in between. In addition, they also had other opportunities available at the time.

> *... at the time I was made redundant... I was offered a job actually... but... the hours, the shifts that they were expecting me to work... and it would have meant travelling up there staying for the week and then just coming back for the weekends and I was not prepared to do that at the time.*

Push versus pull factors

Positive choice entrants clearly experienced more pull factors than either the reluctant recruits or constrained choice entrants. They were able to make a relatively free choice based purely on what they felt self-employment had to offer in comparison to being an employee.

Yet it does not appear that positive choice entrants were motivated by a desire to be self-employed per se. Although they did choose self-employment above other available options, their decisions were not based on long-term aspirations to run a business. In fact, they were highly specific to their circumstances at the time. Crucially, all of them had experienced a 'trigger' which inspired their decision to become self-employed.

For some people, redundancy offered them the opportunity to reconsider their plans and aspirations as well as the financial and psychological freedom to consider a career change. For example, when one positive choice entrant's husband left the air force after serving for 25 years, they perceived themselves to be entering a new phase in their lives and began to consider ways of making changes. At the same time, the annuity her husband had received meant that they had a substantial amount of money to invest. They saw self-employment as an opportunity to invest their windfall and improve the quality of their lives.

Others' decisions were triggered by a 'last straw' at work which made them stop and consider their options. One decided to give up on his hopes for a career within the organisation he had joined when he left school when he realised his commitment to the job was not valued by his employers:

> *I used to put myself out for... little reward... I was high on the work bit, I was happy to do the work, I wanted to do the work so I'd put myself out... Basically... someone with no experience came in at a higher band of pay... so I came to the conclusion, 'Why should I put myself out and not get paid for it?'*

He began to think of other ways to achieve the type of rewards he felt he deserved.

Until they experienced this trigger, positive choice entrants had not considered self-employment. Having been pushed to reassess their circumstances and reconsider their options, they were *pulled* into self-employment, because they perceived it to offer the most advantages. Without the trigger factor it seems unlikely that they would have considered setting up a business at the time they did, if at all.

THE ENTREPRENEURS

People in this category conformed most closely to the traditional stereo-type of self-employed people. However, even within this single category there were three sub-groups of people, each with a slightly different route into self-employment. Some worked in traditionally self-employed occupations; others had developed hobbies into businesses; and the remainder displayed a 'true' entrepreneurial spirit.

Personal characteristics

The entrepreneurs had a wider age range than people in the other three groups, which is not surprising given the differentiation between them. None of them were old enough for their age to be a disadvantage in the labour market. In contrast, some were sufficiently young for youth to be a frustrating barrier to obtaining the level of autonomy and financial renumeration they sought. The majority had dependent children when they started their businesses and this may also have acted as a further spur to self-employment.

Although the entrepreneurs tended to have had the smoothest entry into self-employment, this was not necessarily because they had the most choices available. Many were skilled and experienced in a trade or profession when they set up their businesses and this was, undoubtedly, an advantage. Despite this, most still had quite constrained employment opportunities – due either to the career path they had chosen to follow or their personality traits. This was not because they had little to offer, but usually because they perceived the available jobs to have little to offer *them*.

In short, the decision to move into self-employment was easier for entrepreneurs because they had fewer alternatives which they perceived as being worthy of consideration.

Why did they become self-employed?

Most of the entrepreneurs had entered self-employment simply in the course of pursuing a particular trade or career path. Some, for example a plasterer, a market trader, a taxi-driver and a commission-only sales agent, would have been unable to pursue their career in anything other than self-employment. Others had graduated from trainee or apprentice-ship roles in trades where aspirations to self-employment were very much the norm. These respondents were primarily in retail or hotel management, where success was often indicated by the ability to work independently in self-employment. Their move into self-employment involved very little active decision-making, it was far more a case of natural career progression.

A second group had become self-employed by setting up businesses which they had previously run as hobbies. For example, one man, a teacher by training, had begun making ceramic plates in his spare time as a hobby and had then won a lucrative contract from British Rail to make all the ceramic plates for all their trains.

> *I started by accident... I started doing these little replica plates... so I was running a little part-time hobby business for nearly eight years... when I finished teaching... this side was an opportunity to run my own business...*

Another man had enjoyed buying and restoring luxury classic cars as a hobby. When he became due for a sabbatical from his job he took the opportunity to build this hobby into a full-time concern. Similarly, a trained engineer who made a lot of money selling the pottery he produced as a hobby used the chance to make money from something he enjoyed to 'get out of the rat race'.

> *I'd taken up pottery as an evening class activity and really loved it... and I bought a kiln and a small wheel... and I thought, 'Right, we'll open a craft shop'...*

The third group of entrepreneurs had always actively wanted to be self-employed and aspired to run their own business. These people had never been happy as employees and felt unable to progress. They conformed most closely with the image generally associated with the self-employed. One had demonstrated entrepreneurial tendencies from a very young age:

> *I employed my first person at thirteen... I worked as a butcher's assistant... and the job I didn't like was scrubbing out the boards from the freezer or from the fridge so I actually employed a mate to come in for two and a half hours on a Saturday morning... so I got the pay from the boss then I paid my employee at the same time.*

He moved into self-employment after only a few years as an employee because, as he put it:

> *Basically I was fed up... the wage was pretty low... it was always being on call... possible promotion... was curtailed... I was adamant when I left that I wasn't going to work as an employee any more.*

As well as an inherent desire to be independent and work for themselves, these people also felt stifled as employees. In many respects, their personalities were incompatible with employee status:

> *... it was the whole ethic... what I was trying to do was achieve a slightly different kind of lifestyle... I wanted to get away from having to be told what to do morning noon and night... I don't suppose I was ever able to run my own life... and within a company environment... you've got to slot into the way that everybody else works... I was pulling my hair out.*

Self-employment also had a symbolic significance.

> *I wanted something of mine that I could build, something more... Something I could be proud of inside... Something I could work at and... get something out of and build... Something that I could say 'Yeah, that's mine'.*

They did not enter self-employment simply because it gave them the opportunity to run a particular business but because it gave them the freedom and creativity they aspired to. For them, self-employment was an end in itself. Some had spent a long time investigating the possibilities for entry into self-employment before they eventually found something which they felt would work. One joked:

> *I kept trying things and trying things...as Edison kept trying, was it a thousand times, to make the lightbulb and they said to him, 'Look you've failed seven hundred and ten times', he said, 'No, I found seven hundred and ten times that it doesn't work'... I like to look at myself as doing it the Edison way... I did find something that worked... but I had to try a lot in the meantime...*

Push versus pull factors

Entrepreneurs certainly seem to have been pulled, rather than pushed, into self-employment. Its attractions were perceived to be far greater than those obtainable from employment. Yet their routes into self-employment still challenge traditional perceptions of motivations for becoming self-employed.

The 'hardy individualists' identified in previous research were not overwhelmingly apparent, even among the entrepreneurs. Not all of them became self-employed out of an all-encompassing entrepreneurial spirit. Indeed, some had no choice but to be self-employed as there were no opportunities for them to work as employees. These people might be considered to have been pushed into self-employment. On the whole, however, although some entrepreneurs had limited opportunities to work for other people or had career aspirations that could not easily be fulfilled as employees, most were pulled rather than pushed into self-employment.

THE IMPORTANCE OF ROUTES INTO SELF-EMPLOYMENT

The routes people took into self-employment were an important determinant of both the type of business they set up and the degree of experience and expertise they brought to the enterprise. Further, as we shall see in Chapter Four, these, in turn, had important implications for the problems they faced later on.

Respondents set up very different types of business, according to the circumstances of their entry into self-employment. Reluctant recruits were severely restricted in terms of the type of business they could set up, given their lack of skills, experience and qualifications. As a result, they tended to set-up businesses which they perceived to require little or no skills or previous experience. Some were able to join existing businesses, either family businesses or larger firms on a franchise basis. Others bought small retail outlets – corner shops, grocery stores, newsagents or pubs – where they could simply take over the running of the business rather than build it up from scratch.

These are the 'low value-added service sector activities which tend to have low barriers to entry, but crowded markets and low survival rates' which Meagher et al (1994) identified with the 'new' self-employed. They also had high fixed costs requiring heavy capital investment and offering little control over variable assets.

Constrained choice entrants' skills and work experience meant that they had a wider range of choices when they became self-employed. They were, at least, able to pursue their existing skills and many started businesses in areas in which they had experience. They also, on the whole, set up businesses from which they were likely to gain job satisfaction. One, having spent all his working life as a carpenter, set up a business which gave him the creative freedom to produce higher quality, specialist work. For a golf-obsessed respondent, self-employment offered the chance to pursue his 'passion' on a full-time basis. Although constrained choice entrants were unlikely to make a great deal of money, by starting a business which offered a particular skill or more specialist service they were likely to receive slightly higher returns that the reluctant recruits. More importantly, a few constrained choice entrants had some previous experience of being self-employed.

Positive choice entrants and entrepreneurs tended to set-up higher profile businesses offering quality or specialist services, often in niche markets and promising high financial returns. One opened a musical instrument shop. Another offered a specialist architecture service. Although it may be more difficult to build up a client base for specialised skills or services, once they had managed to do so, it was likely to be more secure. This made them less vulnerable to fluctuations in the economy than the reluctant recruits and some of the constrained choice entrants. In addition, positive choice entrants and entrepreneurs also faced less uncertainty. Most of them were experienced in the work they were pursuing. They were also much more likely than either reluctant recruits or constrained choice entrants to have some previous experience of self-employment or business accounting.

People who set up businesses in areas in which they had previous experience enjoyed multiple advantages. They were not required to 'learn on the job' in the way that reluctant recruits had to. Frequently they had been well respected as employees and could enter self-employment with the confidence that they could provide a good service and build up a sound customer/client base. They also had good business networks to call on. In addition, some were able to 'poach' clients they had served whilst employees to cushion their transition into self-employment.

In addition, a few positive choice entrants and entrepreneurs were able to cushion their move into self-employment even further by running their business alongside full-time employment for a short time either as a hobby or as a going concern. This offered them the opportunity to wait until they were confident that their business was viable before they gave up the security of employment.

Clearly, then, people's routes into self-employment are important in a number of different contexts. It is not simply the fact that the individuals in this study had entered self-employment for such a wide range of reasons and from such a variety of different circumstances, although this is interesting to uncover. More important than the different routes themselves is the extent to which these routes can impact on people's experience of being self-employed. The importance of people's routes into self-employment was reflected in the different types of business which they were able to set up and their level of experience and confidence in running them. Consequently, in many respects the risks associated with being self-employed differ alongside the routes by which people have entered this form of employment.

Chapter 2

Financial Arrangements During Self-employment

Rigorous, well-maintained financial procedures are paramount when individuals set up their own businesses, however small those businesses might be. Clear, accurate records are necessary to prove liability for tax and VAT. They are also essential if people are to be able to monitor their finances and make informed decisions about spending.

For self-employed people, these procudures need to cover both business and personal finances. Unless they have a clear idea of the amount of money coming into and going out of the business, and how this compares to the amount they need for the business to survive, they are unable to assess the viability of their business. Further, unless people calculate the level of income they need to cover their household expenses, they cannot accurately assess the amount of money which is available to keep the business afloat. Anecdotal evidence suggests that many people grossly underestimate the amount of money they need for household expenses and, therefore, often embark on their business with unrealistic expectations of the amount of income they need to generate.

Advice agencies who deal with business problems argue that an essential element of good financial organisation is the strict separation of business and personal finances – both in theory and in practice. Self-employed people often receive *personal* income from sources besides their business. This can include wages earned from other jobs or by other household members, as well as income from investments or state benefits. This personal income should be kept separate from the money coming into the business, from the service or goods it supplies. Likewise personal expenses such as housing costs, household bills, childcare costs, personal discretionary spending and so on need to be separated from the expenditure needed to keep the business afloat, for example, rent or mortgage for the premises, stock, materials, staffing costs and so on.

Maintaining a practical distinction between business and personal finances may seem unnecessary, particularly for single-person enterprises where, to all intents and purposes, income and expenditure are, ultimately, going to and from the same source. In these cases, business and personal income may not, in reality, be that different from each other and it may seem unnecessary and pedantic to insist that each item of business and personal income and expenditure be recorded and managed separately.

In fact, the organisations which advise self-employed people who are encountering difficulties have found that, in many small enterprises, business and personal finances are not kept separately. Rather, anecdotal evidence suggests that business and personal finance often become mixed up in small firms and, further, that personal finance is frequently used to prop up ailing businesses. This means that small business failure is frequently accompanied by significant personal financial losses.

However, very little was known about financial arrangements *during* self-employment and a central aim of this research was to address this gap. A further aim was to understand how and why business and personal finances become entangled and to document the consequences of this confusion.

This has uncovered some important issues in relation to the financial arrangements of people whose businesses were struggling or had failed. A number of factors were associated with this confusion between business and personal finances:

* The boundaries between business and personal finances were often blurred from the outset, as most people had only been able to set up their businesses as a result of huge personal investment.
* People often did not have a clear perception of what it meant to keep business and personal finances separate in practice, although they recognised that they should understand the importance of this distinction in theory.
* Financial problems during self-employment made it very difficult for people to maintain any distinction between business and personal finances, even where they had set out to keep them separate.

This lack of distinction between business and personal finances had important consequences for the impact of small business failure.

SETTING UP AND FINANCING A SMALL BUSINESS

Much of the financial context for self-employment is, in fact, set by financial institutions. In the UK, financial institutions rarely issue loans to people without collateral and few people moving into self-employment have anything to offer other than personal wealth, usually in the form of housing equity. As a result, personal finances were the main

Table 2.1 – *Main sources of finance to set-up a small business*

Source of finance	Number of respondents	Amount of money raised
Secured formal borrowing	23	Minimum – £ 5,000
Unsecured formal borrowing	2	Maximum – £130, 000 Minimum – £ 1,200
Informal borrowing	1	Maximum – £ 5,000 £17,000
Redundancy payments	5	Minimum – £ 2,000
Other sources of personal finance – savings, divorce settlement, annuity, industrial tribunal settlement.	4	Maximum – £ 7,500 Minimum – £ 1,800
Commercial mortgage	1	Maximum – £9000
No set-up costs	4	£ 62,000
Total	40	

source of financing a move into self-employment or starting a small business among the people who took part in the research. In this they were little different from the generality of small business start-ups (Storey and Strange, 1992). This almost always took the form of securing business loans as additional charges on the family home. In this respect, business and personal finances were not separate in the way that they are for people in other forms of employment.

Virtually all the respondents used personal finances to fund their move into self-employment to some degree. But often this was as a supplementary source of finance, with most people relying on commercial borrowing as their main funding source (see Table 2.1). Indeed, more than half of the people we interviewed had raised money for their business by borrowing against the security of their family home. The amounts they raised ranged from £5,000 to £30,000. Only one person had obtained a commercial mortgage and a further two had unsecured loans. The remainder had relied mainly on either redundancy payments or on a range of sources of personal finance, including savings, a divorce settlement, an annuity and compensation awarded by an industrial tribunal.

The distinction between people who had to borrow in order to set up their businesses and those who were able to use their own capital has key implications for the financial circumstances in which respondents embarked on self-employment. Those who had borrowed heavily and, in a few cases unwisely, against the value of their home were committed to making heavy repayments right from the outset. If these repayments were not made, they risked losing their home.

People who borrowed money on an unsecured or informal basis did not face such great financial pressures at the start of their self-employed career. First, because informal and unsecured borrowing tended to relate to smaller amounts of money. Second, because people who had borrowed from informal sources or who were financing their business with an unsecured overdraft usually had a greater degree of flexibility in the timing and nature of repayments.

Clearly, those who did not have to borrow at all to set up their business were in the most favourable financial position when they embarked on self-employment and, subsequently, when their business ran into difficulties.

Routes into self-employment and sources of start-up finance

Chapter 1 notes the significance of routes into self-employment in terms of the type of business respondents set up. Routes into self-employment were equally significant in influencing financial arrangements.

The reluctant recruits, in their need to find businesses for which they required few skills or previous experience, frequently had to buy businesses as going concerns, which usually had very high fixed costs. Consequently, they had to raise a considerable amount of money in order to fund their move into self-employment. The amounts they borrowed were at the higher end of the scale – ranging from £20,000–£130,000. As they had few or no existing financial resources to draw on they had to borrow the whole amount required to set up. Moreover, the only way they could raise the money they needed was to borrow against the equity in their homes.

The few reluctant recruits who managed to move into self-employment without extensive borrowing did so more by necessity than by choice. These were the ones who, because of their age and employment history, were unable to obtain finance from formal sources. Their move into self-employment was governed by the amount of money they could obtain. They either joined existing businesses which required only a small amount of money to 'buy in', or worked as franchisees on a commission-only basis.

Constrained choice entrants, on the other hand, made very different financial arrangements to set themselves up in business. They were more likely to have a skill to sell than reluctant recruits and this often meant that they faced lower start-up costs. Where they did borrow from formal sources they were able to manage on much lower levels of finance than the reluctant recruits and secured loans for respondents in this group ranging from £10,000–£21,000. In addition, some constrained choice entrants had access to redundancy packages which enabled them to set up a business without extensive borrowing.

Positive choice entrants were also often able to set up in self-employment without extensive borrowing. In fact, only half of this group borrowed. Formal borrowing was less significant among this group, with amounts ranging from £5,000–£20,000. Positive choice entrants were more likely to use redundancy payments or other sources of finance, such as a divorce settlement, to set up their businesses. The only person to have obtained a business loan was a positive choice entrant.

Among the entrepreneurs there was an important distinction between those who were pursuing a self-employed trade or profession and the more 'traditional' entrepreneurs. The first group often faced similar financial circumstances to the reluctant recruits when they moved into self-employment. Those who had trained in retail and hotel management, for example, had to purchase a shop or hotel in order to fully realise their ambitions. This required them to borrow significant amounts of money, ranging from £11,000–£65,000 in secured facilities.

In contrast, the more traditional entrepreneurs were able to embark on self-employment either without having borrowed at all, or with a maximum of only £5000. Some, had started very small, as single person operations, often without premises, with the expectation of expansion later on. As a result, they had no significant start-up costs. Others were trading on a skill and therefore only needed to buy the basic equipment which allowed them to operate. In one case a respondent used his long employee career to reduce his start-up costs by 'poaching' some of his clients from employment, beginning his self-employed career with a secure client base and avoiding the cost of advertising and the uncertainty of a slow start.

Problems with start-up finance

Few people had either sought or received any financial advice regarding their move into self-employment. Those who had borrowed formally had interviews with the manager or small business adviser at their bank. However, these meetings were largely to reassure the bank of the security of its investment rather than to scrutinise respondents' approach and method of funding their move into self-employment. As a result, several made inappropriate decisions which had long-term financial consequences for their business. For these people, the general pressures of heavy borrowing were greatly magnified.

Badly timed borrowing

A couple of respondents suffered as a result of poorly timed borrowing, often a direct result of their enthusiasm for self-employment. One, for example, decided to raise the money to set up his business by selling his house and buying a less expensive property. He bought his new house with the help of a £20,000 bridging loan to tide him over. Not only did the crash of the housing market mean that he was unable to sell his old house, it also meant that the value of his new house decreased. Despite this, he had to maintain repayments not simply on his new home but also on his bridging loan.

Another respondent, having found the ideal premises for his new business, obtained a second mortgage on his home and gave up his previous occupation in the expectation of moving straight into self-employment. In the event, however, he was delayed by six months:

> *...I absolutely hated the job and rather stupidly I gave it up. That does sound stupid now but...we'd already seen the shop and it was empty...and they said, 'It'll only take eight weeks to get in, there's nobody else to worry about to move out'...Anyway the remortgage money came through just after Christmas...and by the time everything was eventually sorted out, we...got the keys in about June...*

This had a serious impact:

> *...in all that time the only income we had was the interest on the money that was still in the building society and we weren't earning anything so every bill that came in for six or seven months we had to use the money that was meant for the business...*

In addition, they had to start repaying the second mortgage straight away. This, too, had to be paid out of the money they had borrowed to start the business rather than from their business income, as they had anticipated.

Badly structured finances

Other respondents were also thrown into disarray by 'last minute hitches' in their financial arrangements. However, in their desperation to hang onto their plans and dreams of being self-employed, they ignored these mishaps and went ahead with the business regardless. The effects of these financial time-bombs, which dogged their businesses from the start, proved impossible to recover from.

One woman, relying on an estate agent to organise the finance for the purchase of the shop she wanted to buy, initially agreed to take on a secured loan over ten years requiring monthly repayments of £700. However, 'at the last minute' this funding fell through although she did not fully understand why this had occurred. The estate agent managed to arrange a second loan facility with a different bank but the term of the loan had to be shortened to seven years, which increased the monthly repayments by a further £200. Although this was a serious financial blow she decided to continue with the arrangements because she was '*too far down the line to stop*'.

A second respondent also lost an important element of the funding he had been relying on to set up his business. He, too, decided to go ahead and open the business anyway in the vain hope that the finances could be restructured at a later date. Consequently, the business opened with insufficient funds and badly structured finances. Although, in many ways, the business was successful, it could not withstand these problems. He said:

> ...*we were a success...from people coming through the door, but the trouble was we couldn't fund our borrowing because they weren't structured in the right way.*

As a result, despite its high takings, the business simply 'lurched from one crisis to another' before, eventually, closing down.

In effect, both of these businesses were doomed from the outset.

Discarded advice

More importantly, however, the few respondents who did receive formal advice about their move into self-employment, often paid little heed to it.

In general, the credit boom of the 1980s, coupled with the political and economic support for small businesses, meant that funding for business start-ups was relatively easy to obtain during this period. A number of people in this study spoke of the 'easy money' they encountered when exploring the option of borrowing to move into self-employment. Despite this relaxed lending climate, financial institutions were clearly concerned about lending to some of the respondents in this study. Two were refused bank loans on the grounds that the businesses they were proposing to buy were simply not sound investments. One woman said:

> *I went to [high street bank] and he said 'No way would we consider it'...he was the one [bank manager] I'd been using all the time and he just said it wasn't profitable enough.*

This did not deter them, however. Having tried to obtain finance from several other banks and finance houses she discovered that, aged 53, she was considered too old to be given a mortgage by a bank or building society. Despite these difficulties, she went ahead with buying the business, obtaining a mortgage from a finance house in her daughter's name.

Another was not only refused a loan outright but was also advised against the business he was proposing to buy. With hindsight, he recognised the truth in his bank manager's concerns:

> ...we went to see the manager... and he advised us not to go, not to do it. He said lots of things which have come true since. Our age...; and he said that business was a bit dodgy; and that you couldn't beat working at a place where you get your wage every week...; and had we considered holidays when you've got to find someone to look after the shop...

Yet at the time, he simply dismissed this advice without investigating it further. He said '...we just thought he was being over cautious.' He went on to borrow from a credit company who, he recognised, had a more relaxed attitude to lending the money:

> There weren't a lot of questions asked...they just were very anxious to loan us the money...

He was quite severely disadvantaged by the high interest rates charged by the credit company, in comparison to a bank or building society. In addition, in failing to check the business accounts before agreeing to lend the money, the credit company allowed the respondent to embark on a business which would never be sufficiently profitable to repay the loan.

To recap, then, virtually all of the respondents in this study had invested a significant proportion of their personal wealth and financial security into setting up their business. Given the extent of personal investment in small businesses, it is easier to understand how and why the distinction between business and personal finances may become blurred for many self-employed people. In addition, the vast majority had funded this personal investment by borrowing, usually against the equity in their family home. This created additional financial pressures on the business which were difficult to withstand.

SOURCES OF FURTHER INVESTMENT

Previous studies of small business finance have not investigated financial investment which occurs while the business is running – generally they stop short at documenting the sources and amounts of start-up funds. This research illustrates the significance of continued investment of personal finance to support the running costs of small businesses. Just as personal finances were, more often than not, crucial in funding a business start-up, the extent to which people supported the running costs of their businesses with injections of personal finance was equally significant. They continued to use often large amounts of personal money to keep their business running when the income it generated was insufficient to meet its running costs.

Among respondents in this study, this continued personal investment took two forms. First, further borrowing of large sums of money to invest in the business. Second, much smaller-scale, informal investment on a more frequent basis, for example, paying business expenses on a personal credit card, using personal savings or a spouse/partner's income to buy stock for the business. The formal investment is easier both to document and calculate incidences of further borrowing were usually significant events in respondents' self-employed careers. It is far more difficult to assess the value of the second type of investment, being more frequent and involving smaller amounts of money. However, the real significance of this type of investment was in the nature and extent of its occurrence, rather than in the amounts involved.

Further borrowing

Two thirds of respondents borrowed additional money to keep their business running in the face of financial problems (see Table 2.2). For most, this involved formal borrowing – increasing second charges against their property; taking out personal loans; or obtaining loans for other purposes such as car purchase or home improvements which they then ploughed into the business. Several people also converted large business overdrafts into personal loans to increase the amount of finance available to the business. These respondents had usually borrowed substantially to set up the business in the first place.

A few borrowed from more informal sources, often because they had exhausted their access to formal borrowing facilities. Some were able to obtain substantial amounts in loans from friends and family. In extreme cases, family members obtained secured loans on their properties and passed the money on to respondents. In this respect, the mixing of business and personal finances extended far beyond simply an individual and his/her immediate family.

Table 2.2 – *Main sources of additional investment*

Source of finance	Number of respondents	Amount of money raised
Secured formal borrowing	12	Minimum – £ 3,000 Maximum – £120,000
Secured overdraft facility	5	Minimum – £ 5,000 Maximum – £ 20,000
Unsecured formal borrowing	2	Minimum – £ 5,000 Maximum – £ 12,000
Informal borrowing	6	Minimum – £ 1,000 Maximum – £ 20,000
No further investment	15	

Informal investment

Respondents also supported their businesses with informal personal investment. For example, it was not uncommon for them to use personal credit cards or savings on a 'one-off' basis to pay for stock for their business. Nor was it unusual for them to bear some of the debts from their business, for example, payments that could not be recovered or bills that could not be met, from a personal overdraft rather than run up the more expensive overdraft facility on their business account.

Where respondents had spouses or partners in paid work there was a clear tendency to use their wages to meet as many household expenses as possible and take little or nothing from the business. However, the most common and ongoing form of informal personal investment in small businesses was in forgone wages. Very few people took more than a bare minimum from their business as a wage. A large proportion only drew a personal income from their business to meet specific personal expenses, for example, their mortgage and utility bills, rather than paying themselves a set weekly or monthly amount. One said:

Yeah, we tried not to...take out too much...I've always felt if there's a bill that needs to be paid...you have to run the business in order to be able to afford to pay those bills...we never ever took out too much.

Another respondent, explaining how she worked out her income from the business, said:

It was like bits and pieces... If I needed to pay something then I would take the money from the business but I had to be last. Everything had to be paid out and what was left, if there was anything left, then I would

> *have it to pay specific bills or just to buy food or whatever...I wasn't getting a salary from the business.*

In most cases, this began as a long-term strategy of continual re-investment of forgone wages into the business.

> *I've not taken a lot out of the business, personally, because we did say we'd try for five years to build it up and pump all profits back into the business.*

People clearly did not expect to draw a sufficient personal income from their business to allow for luxuries and they certainly did not expect to be able to save. One said:

> *I enjoyed the work so much that it didn't bother me...I was still thinking...I'll put it [his income] back in... but I never came to the point where I was paying myself back, you know?*

From this perspective, the more money they could keep in the business the better, and this was clearly reflected in people's attitudes to personal income during self-employment. Moreover, forgoing wages was perceived as a highly acceptable strategy and most respondents expected to reinvest their personal income. In the business world this was perceived as a laudable 'long-term business strategy', particularly within the Asian community.

> *...theoretically we're showing the tax people [an income] but practically we work without wages. All Asians do the same...they want to see the business flourish before they take something out of it.*

While forgoing wages was not necessarily problematic in itself, it blurred the distinction between business and personal finances even further. It also meant that business expenses tended to take priority over personal expenses, leaving important domestic bills unpaid in order to maintain the financial stability of the business.

FINANCIAL ARRANGEMENTS DURING SELF-EMPLOYMENT

The sources of finance for small businesses mean that, for many people, business and personal finances are intricately linked from the start of their self-employed career. Further, respondents' commitment to their businesses meant that they were only too willing to boost their business finances with additional injections of finance, generally culled from personal sources. Their desire to take as little money as possible out of the business as wages meant that, from the outset, money which belonged to them, personally, was being used as a source of income for the business. Consequently, for many people, the notion of instigating a separation between business and personal finances was meaningless.

Three key themes emerge from a qualitative analysis of respondents' financial arrangements in self-employment. First, a small group did not perceive any advantages in maintaining a distinction between business and personal finances nor did they perceive there to be any serious disadvantage in mixing them. Second, many others held quite a narrow perception of what it actually meant to mix business and personal finances. As a result, they did not always recognise the extent to which the distinction between their financial arrangements became blurred in practice. Third, the merging of business and personal finances was often the result of the severe financial pressures on self-employed people.

In fact, only two of the 40 respondents managed to keep their business and personal finances separate throughout their self-employed career.

No separation at all

Around a fifth of the people in this study had never tried to separate their business and personal finances. They did not even have separate accounts for business and personal use and kept no separate record of business and personal income and expenditure. All income and expenditure were treated the same way, regardless of whether their source was business or personal. One explained:

> *Basically, I didn't have a bank account, the only bank account I had was my business account. So, everything, personal and business got paid out of that one account.*

For these people, mixing business and personal finances was not perceived as being problematic. In part, this was because they did not fully appreciate the consequences of merging the two. However, they also made a strong case for the fact of keeping a single set of accounts, and believed that dealing with all income and expenditure in the same way was the most logical way of working. They saw little point in trying to make a distinction between business and personal finances. One argued that business and personal finances were '*inextricably linked*' because of the nature of self-employed finance. Another simply did not perceive them to be separate and saw no reason to treat them as such. As he put it: '*It's all still mine.*'

Unacknowledged overlap

Around a third of respondents, however, simply did not recognise the extent to which their business and personal finances overlapped in practice. They often believed, quite erroneously, that they *had* kept their business and personal finances completely separate. They did, indeed, keep separate accounts of income and expenditure from both sources and when asked about their business and personal finances said that they always kept them separate. One explained *'the business was run as a business and whatever was spent on the house was something separate from that.'*

However, this separation was almost entirely a function of accounting procedures rather than a reflection of actual behaviour. In practice, the distinction was far less clear cut. Explaining how they managed their finances, this group of people frequently gave examples of using personal money to maintain their business:

> *We really kept the business afloat by using my savings... I used to take £200 [from the savings account] every Saturday, go down the warehouse and get stuff.*

They also used personal credit cards to give their business greater financial flexibility. One man, who was strongly opposed to credit cards for personal use, obtained a personal credit card solely to improve the cashflow of his business:

> *I wasn't interested in having half a dozen credit cards for using for personal and domestic usage [but]... knowing that I might want short term funds... I used a number of credit card accounts that I had got – personal ones... lined up literally as short term availability of cash.*

Actual money-management was often as haphazard among respondents who thought they maintained a separation as among those who did not recognise any distinction at all.

> *Just on a day-to-day basis...any bills that we incurred we paid for them through the business...we wouldn't account for them but they came out of the business.*

This day-to-day confusion would then be addressed in the written accounts at the end of the week or month so that business and personal expenditure was, at least on paper, kept separate. One person described this process exactly.

> *...I didn't go each week and have a wage packet...or anything. I used to just use a company cheque for going out, if I was going out for a*

*meal I'd just write a cheque out, buy petrol write a cheque out... so the
accountant sort of moved the figures about and said, 'Well, that's your
drawings, that's what you've had out of the company so that's what
you're going to be taxed on'.*

Most of these people did not recognise the difference between having
separate accounting procedures and actually keeping their finances
separate in practice. This was largely the result of a strong tendency to
view the mixing of business and personal finances primarily in terms of
expenditure rather than income or investment. While they would rarely
think of using business income for personal expenditure they did not
display similar qualms about doing the reverse – using personal income
to cover business expenses.

Only a couple of people commented on the difficulty of maintaining
a practical separation between business and personal finances. One
believed that once an individual had invested everything they had in
starting a business *'you just pool what money you've got'*. Another
recognised the tokenism of keeping separate accounts if all the money in
them was from the same source:

*There was a separate bank account, yes, but they'd all been propped
up by me anyway so as far as the money in general is concerned, it's
just one lot of money.*

Enforced merging of business and personal finances

The fact that many small businesses generate very low incomes has been
well-documented in research (see, for example, Meagher et al, 1994). In
this study, even respondents who tried hard to separate their business
and personal finances in practice were often hampered by the financial
pressures that they faced. At the start of their self-employed career, some
did, in fact, keep separate accounts and paid themselves a set wage from
which they met all their personal expenses. At the extremes, one man,
who had two separate but related businesses, charged himself commercial rates when he used the services of one business for the other.

However, many found that their businesses were simply not gener-
ating sufficient income to cover their expenses. The resulting financial
problems, coupled with their credit commitments, meant that the majority had to struggle simply to keep afloat. When faced with these financial
difficulties, the vast majority of people were unable to maintain any sort
of distinction at all between their business and personal finances. One
explained:

> *We started off having a set account for housekeeping, then we finished off with 'Is there any money? Can we spare any money to go shopping with?' It was like that...just taking it out of the takings...we didn't separate it.*

When financial pressures began to mount, they were forced to use whatever money they had to pay their most urgent bills:

> *I had a business account and my own account. We even had a deposit account for your VAT...my plan was...put so much in the private account and put so much in this deposit account...under normal circumstances that would have worked, but we just didn't have the money coming in so we got to the point where I couldn't put any in the private account, I couldn't put any in the other account...I had to start using my own private money to support the business...it was just juggling about really...*

One respondent had to use his personal overdraft to pay his staff's wages. Another often had to rely on his wife to pay off business debts from her income as an employee. One couple were even forced to use the money they had been saving for the baby they were expecting.

> *...we had a little building society book... and we used to put £30 a week away for him and in the end we had to draw the lot out one week. We had no money...and it broke out hearts to do it, because that was all his little savings.*

Diverting income from personal use to support the business meant that respondents then faced a whole range of mounting domestic bills. When this occurred they began to simply use *'whatever money we had to pay whatever needed paying'*. Financial arrangements became increasingly difficult to separate:

> *I mean it was that closely interlinked that the debts, it would have been impossible to separate...where the debts came from...I wouldn't like to try to separate them at all.*

As one person put it, in these circumstances *'every need becomes a priority, it's not important who pays what, only that it gets paid'*. As a result, they quickly lost track of all aspects of their finances. One described his efforts to try and cope.

> *Rob Peter to pay Paul...It seems logical and it works to start with, but it can't for ever.*

In more extreme cases, where business income was very low, other members of respondents' families, usually their partners, began to use their own money to try and support the business. One person explained:

> *In that situation...you've got...to try and survive....He's [respondent's partner] going out earning money, but you're using his money to stave off the debtors that you've got because at the end of the day, your husband's responsible for what debts you're in...*

Crucially, once people had started mixing business and personal finance it became virtually impossible to stop.

WHY DO BUSINESS AND PERSONAL FINANCES BECOME MIXED UP?

It is not possible to identify any factors which completely explain why business and personal finances become confused as so much of the confusion relates to the context of self-employment. However, this analysis highlights a number of factors which are key indicators of the potential for confusion to occur. These include:

* routes into self-employment;
* previous experience;
* financial aspirations;
* home-working;
* structure of the business;
* financial commitments;
* advice and support with accounts.

Routes into self-employment

There was some correspondence between respondents' routes into self-employment and their financial arrangements while trading. Those who never tried to separate their business and personal finances were mostly reluctant recruits. The two respondents who successfully maintained a distinction between business and personal finances throughout their self-employed career were both entrepreneurs. The others fell between these two extremes.

Clearly there is a logic behind this relationship. The reluctant recruits had become self-employed as a last resort because it offered the only opportunity to be in paid work. They had very little control over their decision to become self-employed, little time for research or planning and little choice over the type of business they set up.

The other categories of respondents – constrained choice, positive choice and entrepreneurs – despite having different routes into self-employment, were similar in some important respects. They enjoyed a greater degree of control over their decision to enter self-employment and had more opportunity to consider the move before it became a reality. Subsequently, they had a firmer knowledge base from which to run a business when they started out. They were, at least, aware that business and personal finances should be kept separate.

It seems, then, that reluctant recruits, are the most susceptible to mixing business and personal finances due to a lack of awareness of the importance of keeping them separate. However, other factors must also be taken into consideration. If financial arrangements during self-employment could be explained simply in relation to routes into self-employment we would expect all entrepreneurs, positive choice and constrained choice entrants to be relatively successful in keeping business and personal finances separate and all reluctant recruits to be unsuccessful. Yet this was not always the case. There are clearly other important influences at work.

Previous experience

Experience of self-employment and running a business was a very important factor, influencing not simply how respondents made their financial arrangements but also suggesting why they did so. So, too, was previous experience as an employee in the chosen area of self-employment. In particular, this experience was central in explaining higher rates of successful financial management among some reluctant recruits and constrained choice respondents than would, perhaps, have been anticipated. Conversely, it was also useful in providing a better understanding of the reverse – lower rates of success among the entrepreneurs and positive choice respondents than might otherwise have been expected.

People who had never tried to keep their business and personal finances separate were inexperienced both in the businesses they ran and in self-employment. In many respects, they simply lacked the knowledge and experience necessary for effective financial planning. Those who understood the importance of keeping business and personal finances separate, on the other hand, were either more experienced in self-employment and running a business or needed very little experience to get by.

The majority of respondents who tried to keep some distinction between business and personal finances had some experience of the business that they were running, even though they had not previously been self-employed. Consequently, they recognised that they were working in a different context which prompted them to think more carefully about their financial arrangements. Many of these respondents also had some awareness of the financial side of the work they were doing, even though they had not previously been responsible for the finances.

Financial aspirations

Respondents' attitudes to self-employment and money were also an important indicator of their likely approach to business and personal finances. In particular, the extent to which financial gain was a significant 'push' factor in becoming self-employed was a central influence on their financial arrangements.

Most of the people who never tried to separate their business and personal finances had given little consideration to the financial side of their business. These were primarily the reluctant recruits whose commitment was simply to being in paid work, rather than to self-employment. None of the reluctant recruits expressed any interest in or awareness of their potential earning capacity in self-employment. They treated their entry into self-employment very much as they would have reacted to starting a new job as an employee – their primary concern simply being to earn enough money to make ends meet.

The few positive choice entrants and entrepreneurs who did not separate business and personal finances were also not financially motivated. They had become self-employed primarily because it offered the opportunity to pursue a particular type of work. One, for example, had become self-employed to get away from the rigorous structure imposed by employee status and, primarily, valued the freedom that self-employment gave him to pursue his artistic creativity. He commented:

> I think we were living on so little at the time that we didn't think we could get much worse. We'd always lived on the edge of poverty. I've never had much money in my life at all, I don't think I ever will, you know. If I've got £5 in my pocket or 5 pence, it doesn't really bother me.

Another respondent had left countless jobs to find an opportunity to pursue a particular type of work which was only possible through self-employment.

In contrast, the respondents who *did* recognise the importance of keeping business and personal finances separate tended to express a greater awareness of the potential to 'do well' financially from self-employment. One constrained choice entrant explained:

... you always hear about people doing well in businesses, they're making lot of money and that sort of thing, so we decided we might make a good living out of it.

Other positive choice entrants had left quite highly paid employment with the expectation of significant financial rewards from self-employment. For them, putting financial structures in place to keep track of the money they were making was a key element of their entry into self-employment.

Home-working

Self-employed people are particularly vulnerable to confusion between their business and personal finances if they work from home (Birmingham Settlement, 1991). Because they share business and domestic premises, these people immediately encounter a potential confusion of business and personal finances. For example, the cost of the business premises is combined with domestic housing costs. How does one distinguish between the heat, light and water used for the business and that used for normal domestic consumption?

Rigorous business accounting demands that, in these circumstances, an accountant should work out the proportion of each bill which should be covered by the business and that which remains the self-employed person's personal responsibility. In theory, this allows the boundaries between business and personal to be strictly drawn and avoids confusion regarding which bill should be paid from which account.

Yet this may be unrealistic in practice. Most of the people in our sample did not employ an accountant. This is particularly likely to be the case for the low-income self-employed. Further, even where this procedure is followed in theory, it does not preclude a mixing of business and personal finances in practice. Finally, when under financial pressure, self-employed people faced with a single set of bills for combined business and personal use are even more likely to simply pay the whole bill with whatever money they have, rather than calculate the proportions which should be paid from each account. This issue is of increasing concern as a special survey of self-employed people in 1987 found that home-based working accounted for around 78 per cent of all self-employed businesses (Hakim, 1989).

The vulnerability of self-employed people who work from home was illustrated by this study. People whose business and domestic premises were combined were far less likely to distinguish between business and personal finances than other respondents. They usually received only one set of bills relating to both their home and business.

Further, they were often happier dealing with the bills in this way as they saw little logic in making separate arrangements.

Structure of the business

For some of the people in the study, rigorous financial organisation was more of a practical necessity than for others, due to the structure of the businesses they were involved in.

Those who never tried to separate their business and personal finances were all sole traders, without other business partners or employees. They were also not receiving any household income other than that generated by their business. As a result, the distinction between business and personal finances was, in practice, much less real. By and large, all the money that came into the business or household did, ultimately, belong to the respondent, as did any money going out. Although, in an ideal world, keeping business and personal money separate would have allowed them to gauge profit and loss more accurately, in effect, they did not need rigorous accounting procedures to obtain this information – they could simply look at the amount of money they had overall.

On the other hand, those who had other household income – from a job as an employee, another business or other household members – were much more likely to recognise the importance of separating their business from their personal finance. Similarly, the distinction between business and personal finances was also important for people who had either a business partner or employees. These situations created a necessity for keeping a clear account of all income and expenditure that, occasionally, even overcame the drawbacks of lack of experience or insufficient opportunity for preparation and planning.

Financial commitments

The amount of money people had invested in setting up their business and the source they had obtained the money from was also influential.

Those whose financial commitments put them under heavy financial pressure from the outset tended to be much less successful in separating business and personal finances than those who were under less pressure. People who had borrowed extensively, sometimes from more than one source, were under huge pressure to make substantial repayments right from the day that they started their businesses. This was particularly so when the source of finance put their homes under threat if they did not maintain repayments. Their primary focus, then, was to ensure that these repayments could be met somehow. Often they had very little time or opportunity to establish systematic financial procedures before they began to struggle financially.

On the other hand, people who had made smaller initial investments into their businesses or who had been able to avoid heavy borrowing managed, at least initially, to keep their business and personal finances more distinct. In fact, the two respondents who succeeded in maintaining the distinction between their business and personal finances, despite business difficulties, had no set-up costs whatsoever. Both had started with very small businesses which they had built up gradually as they became more secure financially. As a result, they had much more control over their finances throughout the period of their self-employment and this was reflected in their financial organisation.

Advice and practical support

Having someone to advise and help with the books and accounts for the business was a key indicator of the likelihood of self-employed people making a separation between their business and personal finances. This related not simply to formal advice received from an accountant or business advisor but also to informal support as well. The most important factor of all, however, was having someone, other than the owner of the business, taking responsibility for keeping the business accounts.

Respondents who never tried to separate their business and personal finances had rarely sought advice on how to manage their accounts before they started their businesses. Similarly, few received advice while they were trading and none of them had any informal support with their accounts from friends and family. The onset of financial problems, which often hit people very early on in their self-employed career, then precluded the option of employing professional accountants. One remarked:

> *I think most accountants are quite useful...[but] the trouble is with accountants it costs a fortune in money and I wasn't in the game for paying x pound an hour to go and have advice from the accountant.*

Consequently, they did not have access to anyone who could advise them on accounting procedures or help them translate procedure into practice. Nor did they have anybody to notice their mistakes or warn them of potential problems.

In contrast, almost all the respondents who made some attempt to separate business and personal finances had received advice in managing their accounts. Often this was from accountants or local business networks, or else from friends or family members who were or had been self-employed.

However, a further distinction can be made between respondents who simply received advice with their accounts and respondents who had another person who was responsible for managing the books and accounts. This was the crucial deciding factor in whether or not respondents were able to make a real, or simply a paper, distinction between business and personal finances. The evidence suggests that simply having access to someone who could advise people on what they *should* be doing was not enough to ensure good financial practice. What was important was having a third party to monitor financial decision-making to ensure that a distinction between business and personal finances was maintained in practice.

The people who were most successful in keeping their business and personal finances separate, for at least some part of their trading time, usually had a spouse who took care of all the book-keeping for the business. Not only did this relieve them of the time and effort needed to keep accounts up-to-date, but it also meant that their financial organisation was exposed to a scrutiny that those who kept their own books lacked. In particular, people whose spouse was involved in keeping the books were clearly more accountable in terms of their use of personal money for business purposes.

THE CONSEQUENCES OF MIXING BUSINESS AND PERSONAL FINANCES

As the organisations which deal with the problems experienced by self-employed people suggest, the consequences of mixing business and personal finances can be very harsh. Self-employed people are significantly disadvantaged by this practice if their business encounters financial difficulties. Where business and personal finances are not distinct, financial problems in one area automatically have knock-on effects on the other. While these effects are not completely avoidable where business and personal finances are kept separate, they are less likely to occur. Where business and personal finances are mixed and a small business fails, self-employed people stand to lose much more than just their source of income.

When respondents lost track of their financial situation they were frequently unable to recognise the point at which they should have stopped borrowing and spending. As a result, they often carried on desperately ploughing money into the business even after they had exhausted all their personal funds. One respondent said of his last few months in business:

> *I was basically using [the] bank's money to live...Don't ask me where the money came from, I haven't got a clue...I just used to write cheques out and just hope they'd be paid.*

At best they ran up serious personal debts as well as business debts. One respondent who was still trading at the time of the research but whose business was in serious financial difficulties explained how personal debts build up when business and personal finances are allowed to merge:

> *The mortgage hasn't been paid this month, the payment on the car hasn't been paid, the insurance hasn't been paid, pension or life insurance hasn't been paid, virtually all the...I mean we sat down and worked it out at the beginning of the month. We had about £2,400 worth of bills to pay – domestic and business – we should have over £2,600 coming in this month and we've had approximately £700. So nothing's got paid, you know.*

Another reflected on the same process:

> *Yes, we always kept the business side of things absolutely up-to-date to the detriment of the personal side of things...We should have let the business side suffer.*

At worst, they risked losing their home, because mortgage arrears had built up as a result of diverting all available money to the business. A number of respondents in this study were actually threatened with mortgage repossession before the full extent of their financial problems fully hit home. For one, this was a particularly bitter pill. She had diligently continued to pay the mortgage on her family home, making this the priority bill and ensuring it was paid at any cost. However, the other debts she had incurred while trying to maintain her business were so great that, when it failed, she was still unable to avoid repossession because their home had been used as security.

> *...we paid the mortgage more or less up until the end, and we went to court and the judge said 'Well, it's repossession because of the collateral'.*

With hindsight, a number of people recognised the mistakes they had made and identified the mixing of business and personal finances as a key contributor to the problems faced by the self-employed:

> *If it's a limited company in today's strict laws...you can't really get into that mess because your accountant has got to advise you that you shouldn't pay your own personal Barclaycard with a limited company*

cheque book. Whereas in the past when I was doing it, nobody really ever said anything...it's still allowed to be very lackadaisical in private business...and most people running their own businesses haven't got a clue how to run a business really.

The financial impact of small business failure is discussed fully in Chapter 4.

Chapter 3

Small Business Failure

The specific reasons why small businesses encounter difficulties and, ultimately, cease to trade are well documented in other studies of self-employed people. The purpose of this research extends beyond a recognition of the factors which cause small business failure, to provide an in-depth understanding of the process by which it occurs. This process incorporates not simply the specific factors which lead to insurmountable problems, but also the whole set of circumstances around small business failure which influence the way in which it impacts on the individuals involved.

Twenty-seven of the 40 respondents in this study had closed their businesses by the time the research took place. The rest were still trading although some still had very serious financial problems. The difficulty many people had in actually admitting business failure, both to themselves and to others, is reflected in the fact that three respondents who had, in fact, gone bankrupt insisted on classifying themselves as 'still trading' because they had managed to sell their businesses as going concerns.

People's experiences of self-employment and the circumstances in which they made the decision to close down were crucial in shaping the impact of business failure. A number of factors were of particular importance, including:

- the lead-up to and reasons for closure;
- the length of time it took respondents to move from the point of serious business problems to the point of closure; and
- the ultimate outcomes of closure.

People commonly struggled to keep their businesses going for as long as they possibly could, often until they were actually forced to close. They rarely decided to simply 'call it a day' on the grounds that the business was no longer profitable or economically viable.

Consequently, small business failure was not, in most cases, a single event but the culmination of a very long process of anxious reflection and desperate negotiation. In this respect, small business failure can predate closure by months or even years. Indeed, many of the businesses which were still trading at the time of this research could still be termed as 'failing', because they had embarked on the process of failure well in advance of our interviews with them. During this process of business failure, respondents had to try to come to terms with letting go of both their financial as well as their personal commitment to the business. The most serious difficulties usually arose from the latter.

SMALL BUSINESS FAILURE: THE CONTEXT

Business problems are, to a large degree, simply part of the reality of running a small business and most of those interviewed for this study could name more than one serious problem which they felt had led to the closure of their business. Many had experienced a 'domino effect', whereby a relatively minor initial problem had escalated, with serious consequences. But in many cases, these problems need not necessarily have resulted in closure. A number of key factors can be identified which set the context for small business failure and were equally important contributory factors to the ultimate necessity to close. These were:

- routes into self-employment;
- people's ability to cope with running a business;
- the nature of the business they were running; and
- financial circumstances.

It was these factors which undermined their ability to cope with the types of problem which are an integral part of self-employment and which made them particularly vulnerable to failure.

Routes into self-employment

Obviously, given the nature of the sample for this study, the majority of respondents' businesses had closed or were failing at the time of interview. Just over a quarter of the people we interviewed were still trading at the time of the research. However, some key themes emerge from a closer analysis of respondents and their businesses.

Far more of the entrepreneurs were still trading at the time of the research than people from other categories of our typology. Virtually all of the reluctant recruits and positive choice entrants, and over half of constrained choice entrants had had to close their businesses. Further, reluctant recruits, constrained choice and positive choice entrants fell victim to circumstances leading to business closure much more quickly than entrepreneurs. The vast majority of people from these three groups closed their businesses within five years. In fact, a disproportionate number closed within the first three years of trading. Entrepreneurs' businesses, on the other hand, had traded for between six and seventeen years before they closed. Clearly, they were better equipped to deal with self-employment and business problems than other groups.

The prognosis for people who were still trading at the time of the research, despite business problems, were also interesting. The outlook was much bleaker for reluctant recruits and constrained choice entrants than it was for either positive choice entrants or entrepreneurs. People in the first two groups who continued to trade had not managed to overcome their business problems. Rather, they were continuing to trade despite business problems because they had too much to lose to do otherwise. Further, they were not optimistic about their chances of avoiding business failure in the future.

For example, one reluctant recruit, who was running a small newsagents and grocery store, had been struggling for seven years. His situation was not improving. He had received advice and support from a specialist advice agency, yet his business was continuing to deteriorate. He was desperate to avoid the stigma of business failure, but knew he faced little option in the long-term other than closure. Similarly, a constrained choice entrant who had been running a specialist sports shop for six years longed to be able to close the business and move on, but was tied to the business by a seven year lease. His lack of business experience meant that he had not recognised the implications of signing such a long lease. He faced serious financial losses from reneging on the terms of the lease. Consequently, unless he could sell the lease he planned to simply 'hang on', losing money, until he was free to leave.

Positive choice entrants and the entrepreneurs, however, who were still trading tended to be much more positive about their future prospects. One entrepreneur was clearly confident of success. He had contacted a specialist advice agency when he felt he could no longer cope alone. The advice and practical support they offered *'gave him the courage'* to pull his business out of a serious decline. In recognition that the market he was aiming at had reached saturation point, he was diversifying his service:

> *...we're offering new services...to approach a wider market. We intend to carry on looking at the type of customers we've already got and sort of expand and build on that – either with existing services, new services or both...*

He was approaching this with enthusiasm:

> *I always maintained, while ever the contracts were coming in or while ever my customers were happy with the service I was giving and the phone kept ringing, I'd keep on.*

Another entrepreneur, who had seriously over-committed himself during his first few years of trading, had scaled down his business after receiving advice. Although he was still encountering some difficulties he was able to work around them and was confident that the upturn in his business would continue. He planned to have repaid all his debts within three or four years, after which he could begin to expand again. Further, he felt that dealing with his business problems had been a valuable learning experience which would enable him to deal more effectively with business problems in the future. He said, *'Oh yeah, it's been the biggest learning point of my life I'd say.'*

Coping with self-employment

Another key contributory factor to small business failure among people in this study was the fact that they were largely unprepared for the harsh reality of self-employment. Most had no experience at all of running a business. Others had unrealistic expectations of what it would be like to be self-employed. In short, self-employment often fell far short of the idyll that the stereotypical image of self-employment had led them to expect.

Several people commented on their inexperience and naivety when they set up their business. Their lack of training and business skills posed a much bigger problem than they had anticipated. Some were so constrained or unrealistic in their decision-making that they often found themselves 'stranded' with little or no idea of how to actually run a business. One said:

> *When I actually took over I didn't know anything at all about the business. I'd never worked and never experienced self-employment...I had no idea of what I was actually making out of the business. I knew at the end of the day we were ticking over day-by-day, day-by-day, whether I was making anything or not I didn't know...*

Another who thought he had prepared himself by taking a business course said:

> *...there's the theory and there's the practical. The theory and the practical don't always match up...I mean all those things that I'd leant...had I applied them here I would have hit the wall straight away...Everything that I learnt and believed to be what business was, backfired on me and I was left...isolated.*

As a consequence, he recalled:

> *I made a tremendous amount of mistakes, mistakes that sometimes, when you think about it, most people would have ended up committing suicide over. I made a lot of mistakes over the years...because of my inexperience.*

Lack of experience also meant that, in their enthusiasm to get the business off the ground, they frequently took on too much, too quickly. One remarked:

> *I think 'we ran before we could walk' would be the expression.*

This lack of experience had a profound impact on respondents and had serious consequences for their businesses.

Often, the people who were most seriously disadvantaged by inexperience were those who had become self-employed because it enabled them to pursue a particular skill, rather than because they had any real aspirations to run a business or skills in doing so. For example, a respondent who had enjoyed a very successful career as an architectural metal worker encountered problems very early in his self-employed career. Although he was very good at his job and his ability had enabled him to progress as an employee, it did not, in any way, equip him for the business skills he would need in self-employment. He saw this as his major downfall:

> *I think the main problem with the business has probably been myself. First of all I'm a craftsman, a tradesman and not really a good businessman.*

Another man, a skilled carpenter, found it difficult to adapt to self-employment because it changed the boundaries within which he worked. As an employee his main concern had been doing a *good* job. In self-employment he had to be equally, if not more, concerned with doing a *profitable* job. He found this very difficult to get used to:

> *I'm too easy-going myself and you know, I don't sort of try hard enough to get the best out of every job, financially. I'm more intent on producing a first class job for them rather than a profit.*

People who had managed to continue to trade, despite business problems, were much more likely to have had some business skills which equipped them for self-employment in a way that simply being good at a particular job did not.

Lack of practical experience relevant to running a business was primarily a problem cited by reluctant recruits and constrained choice entrants. However, those with other routes into self-employment also occasionally felt that they had landed themselves in a situation where they had a business to run with none of the skills necessary to do so. One positive choice entrant who had run his business quite successfully as a lucrative hobby found pursuing it as his main occupation, on a full-time basis, was a very different matter:

> *...a very large factor in my failure... was a lack of experience of doing real business, with people who are well versed in it and... who know how to rip you off. In other words naivety, lack of experience. There is no... gentle way to ease in.*

Even some of the positive choice entrants and entrepreneurs found that they simply had not appreciated the skills that were necessary to run a business.

> *I'm an organiser and my organisation and my general overview was... in most respects spot on. But the... business acumen was totally missing.*

Lack of experience was not simply important in relation to people's practical ability to run a business. It was also extremely significant in terms of their ability to cope, physically and psychologically, with being self-employed. In most cases, they had entered self-employment, as one person put it, '*as a romantic dream*'. They often found that the physical and emotional commitment required to run a small business was far greater than they had anticipated. For the first time, they were solely responsible for all the decisions that had to be made in relation to the business and, further, had to bear the consequences of their decision-making. They frequently found this total responsibility difficult to manage. One remarked:

> *I was working literally one hundred and sixty eight hours a week. I was working in the office, I was on call. I used to come home and I'd probably be home ten minutes, may not even have been able to do my dinner, phone would ring 'You've got a problem at such and such a site' and whoosh, out I'd go. I could be out until three, four o'clock in the morning and I still had to be back in the morning.*

Another commented:

> *Well, you weren't allowed to be ill. When you're behind the bar, you know, you've got to go down if you're at death's door... The book work used to get on your nerves... you wanted to be downstairs behind the bar and you could've done without it...*

The physical isolation of running a business was also a problem for some:

> *... the one thing that got me most... is that it's all a one man band. If you're sitting in that chair of control, you're basically responsible for everything... When you look around, although people pretend to be there to help you... there's nobody there.*

Most of the people in our study found running a business was much more of a physical and emotional strain than they were prepared for. Even those with previous experience of self-employment, who were in a better position to predict the problems they were likely to face, were often unrealistic in estimating their ability to cope.

Type of business

In addition to their inexperience, some people were further disadvantaged by the types of businesses they set up. This primarily affected reluctant recruits and constrained choice entrants, who were forced to enter high-input low-return business such as small retail outlets and pubs. However, some positive choice entrants and entrepreneurs also set up businesses in relatively vulnerable service sector activities, for example, in the leisure industry or selling luxury goods.

The vulnerability of these businesses to recessionary pressures is clear. Businesses which were dependent on a large number of customers usually spending quite small amounts of money, such as the grocery stores, corner shops and newsagents that many of the reluctant recruits and constrained choice entrants set up, were unable to withstand a sustained drop in trade. One respondent explained it:

> *I wouldn't wish it on my worst enemy because, you know,... you just sit in your shop waiting for someone to come through that door, and you can do all the promotionals and you can go out on the road touring, we did all that. We did everything but at the end of the day, it's the people who come through the shop door... and it just stopped.*

Others, who had businesses in the leisure industry, such as hotels and catering, or selling luxury goods, such as classic cars, were also hit very hard. They did not experience a gradual decline in trade, which they may have been able to reverse, but a sudden and absolute drop in custom. Their businesses were not able to withstand the impact of this:

> *For about a couple of years I was okay... and then the recession really bit... we were doing nothing... You'd sometimes get a good week... but*

> *you weren't making anything... I mean we had weeks where we'd had
> nobody at all in, you know, and your bills are still going just the same.*

Another respondent described the sudden change in his fortunes very
eloquently:

> *... a very simple fact is that when the risk is being taken during a period
> of expansion and rising, rapidly rising markets, it is difficult for people
> to get an instinct, when the game of musical chairs is on, for when the
> music's going to stop.*

People whose businesses were still trading at the time of the research
had been insulated, to an extent, from the effects of the recession. They
tended to be offering more specialised skills or services such as design
engineering, pottery-making, plastering and so on. They were better
placed to survive the recession because they had developed niche
markets. Although they tended to be reliant on a smaller client base,
they were able to make more money per client or customer than, for
example, those running general stores. In addition, people who were
running businesses in trades such as plastering or pest control were offering a service that people could not easily do for themselves, however
much they may have wanted to save money.

Financial situation

Another key factor in determining which respondents' businesses failed
and which were able to continue trading was the extent to which they
depended on the money from their business for a personal income. Those
who were still trading were much more likely to have a partner in full-
or part-time paid employment. This additional household income
afforded them greater flexibility in deciding the outcome of the business
in two respects. First, they could use this income to support the household while they waited to see if the business would improve. Second, as
Chapter 2 illustrates, they could also use the money to prop up the
business and '*buy themselves out of trouble*' for a while. This was clearly
an important factor in enabling some people to remain in self-employment, despite their business problems.

Discussing how he had been able to keep going despite severe financial problems, one man said:

> *... all our living expenses are paid out of my wife's salary... we've had
> to sit down... and we've kind of sorted out what the wife can afford and
> she's took all the personal stuff and I'm just trying to work to get myself
> out of debt with the business.*

Those whose businesses had failed had not had this flexibility and, as a consequence, had been unable to buy the time to get out of trouble. When they were trying to support their whole household with the money they were making from their business, they did not have the luxury of time to wait for things to improve.

SMALL BUSINESS FAILURE: THE EMOTIONAL STRUGGLE

Overwhelmingly, the people in our study tended to struggle on in self-employment, long after the point at which their business was no longer viable financially. Very few based their decision to close on a rational assessment that it was time to 'cut their losses'. The decision to close down a small business was rarely an economic one and most people continued to trade long after their businesses ceased to be economically viable. This was because their emotional attachment to the business was, in fact, stronger than their financial commitments. Consequently, the decision to close was, primarily, very emotional. Much of the action, or inaction, which characterised the last stages of business failure had emotional motivations. As a result, by the time that their businesses closed, people had not simply generated significant business and personal debts but were also emotionally drained and exhausted.

Virtually all of the people interviewed for this study, regardless of the circumstances of their entry into self-employment, demonstrated high levels of emotional commitment to self-employment in general and to their own business in particular. When talking about their business they often used very emotionally-loaded language. One, who had lost his 14-year-old daughter in a drowning accident said his business was '*like another child*'. Another candidly admitted to using the business as a way of coping after the death of his wife:

> The company literally did replace the wife. I was married on April 2nd 1982 and on October 26th 1982 my wife died, so we was only seven months married. I was out on duty the night she died so I did literally bury myself in the work.

This strong emotional attachment meant that they were sometimes unable to make objective judgements about their businesses. When faced with problems which threatened the whole foundation of their business, they found it almost impossible to take a rational perspective.

Respondents themselves frequently pointed out the absence of logic in their behaviour around the time they were considering whether or not to close the business. One described his actions as being tantamount to *'financial suicide'*. Another was, with hindsight, incredulous at some of the things he had done, which had made his situation much worse than it need have been. Yet he remained unable to explain or rationalise his actions:

> *I threw away the house which could have actually saved the business for me. But it's a very strange business. I can't give you a totally analytical view of all this... Who can say why you do crazy things? You just do.*

A key element of this emotional struggle was the difficulty that most people had in admitting that the problems they were experiencing were, in fact, irresolvable. They employed often elaborate avoidance strategies which avoided them having to face the decision. Frequently this included hiding letters from banks and creditors so as not to have to admit the problems to their families and even to themselves.

> *... when things were at the worst... I'm sure a psychologist has got a name for it... I went through a phase where I could not open envelopes which were obviously related to money. You can read envelopes, I can tell you, without opening them – who they're from and what it's about.*

Even when they were able to admit to the gravity of their business problems, they still found it very hard to finally give up and admit defeat. They frequently continued to trade long after the point at which they had come to terms with the fact that the business was no longer economically viable, in the hope that the situation would improve:

> *Mmm, well this is where you start to chase fool's gold... Oh, you'll get the business back at Christmas, New Years... but the basic damage had been done.*

Respondents were, again, very candid and quite emotional in discussing their reasons for this. They frequently said that they had hung on because of their love for their businesses. Their personal and emotional commitment to the business was so strong that many simply could not conceive of letting it go. They found the thought of losing something in which they had invested so much, and with which they identified so strongly, very hard to take. Some likened the thought of closing their business to a bereavement.

This level of emotional attachment to their businesses had a profound influence over when and how people finally decided to close them down.

CLOSING A SMALL BUSINESS

It is clear, then, that people had to come to terms with the idea of business failure before they could even begin to think about the practicalities of closure. This psychological acceptance was usually a lengthy and emotionally draining process. Consequently, it was in these circumstances that they faced the practical ordeal of going about actually closing the business down. Two main themes emerge from an analysis of respondents' decision-making around closing their businesses.

A very small group were *consolidators* who closed their businesses by choice to cut their losses. The majority, however, were *strugglers* who were prepared to hang onto their businesses for as long as possible, at almost any cost. These people were simply waiting until they were overtaken by events which forced them to close. In this way, they avoided the trauma of actually making the decision to close.

The consolidators

Despite their emotional investment in self-employment and their businesses, the consolidators made strategic decisions to close their businesses, in recognition that their situation was irredeemable. They perceived business closure as the best way to wipe the slate clean and start again. Consolidators came from all routes into self-employment but shared some common characteristics.

They were all men, and most were at the older end of the age spectrum – aged in their late 40s and early 50s. Consequently, however strong their commitment to their business, they recognised that they were too old to be tied to a pipe dream which was not sustainable. They had to start thinking about retirement and, however poor their prospects of finding paid employment, they had to start looking for alternatives.

Further, and most importantly, all of them had something positive to hold on to which eased the blow of closing the business. This took various forms. For a young Asian man who had been forced into self-employment by family pressures, closing the business offered the prospect of escape from self-employment and a chance to resume his education. A positive choice entrant who had set up a business selling and servicing office equipment, closed it down in recognition of the fact that his financial situation was unlikely to improve in the current economic climate:

> *I couldn't carry on the business because of the financial side. I was getting deeper and deeper and at the end of the day I wouldn't have been able to get out of it.*

He was anxious not to get into a situation which would have long-term repercussions that might prevent him setting up another business in the future. Recognising that he could sell his customer base to another company, it was also important for him to act before this was eroded by the recession. This had enabled him to close his business without any debts, and he planned to wait for an upturn in the economy and then start up again.

Two other people had second businesses, which they were running in conjunction with their failing businesses. Prompt closure of their struggling businesses served two practical and positive purposes. First, it ensured that financial problems in one business would not escalate to the point where they posed a threat to the other. Second, it freed up time and money that could then be used to insulate their more successful businesses from the threat of recession.

More important, however, was the fact that business closure represented far less of an admission of failure for the consolidators than for others in the study, and they were all able to identify external factors, rather than poor management, as the reason for the business problems they experienced. This made the idea of closing the business much easier for them to accept. One of them, for example, had traded very successfully for 15 years before health problems eroded his ability to manage his business. Another had always believed his chances of success were hampered by foul play on the part of his previous employer. A third person's business had fallen into serious financial difficulty because, unbeknown to him, his partner had been using company money to support his gambling addiction.

Finally, all of the consolidators had sought and received advice about the specific problems they were facing before they made any decisions about the future. This was a crucial factor in their decision-making. Having sought advice, they were in a much better position to consider their alternatives realistically and decide on their best option. As a result of the advice they had received, they were fully aware of the advantages of closing down at an early stage rather than trying to 'trade their way out' of problems. They were able to cut their losses, secure in the knowledge that this was their best option, before their situation deteriorated to the extent that they had no choice over when and how to close.

The strugglers

The vast majority of people in the study, however, simply struggled on, either until they were too exhausted to continue or until there was nothing left to fight for. They had frequently recognised the prospects of failure quite early in their self-employed career but ignored the signs in the hope that the situation would improve. They were often very honest about the point at which they *should* have given in and closed the business, but had refused to consider it. While these 'head in the sand' tactics enabled them to avoid facing reality, it also meant that their circumstances had often worsened considerably before they finally acknowledged how bad things had become:

> *I have to say that from time to time I became uneasy. I think there's no doubt that, in my case, a large part of making things worse was the classic burying your head in the sand and hoping everything will be okay later on.*

People whose businesses had simply declined gradually, frequently maintained these avoidance tactics for some time:

> *We'd sort of have two reasonable weeks, or one reasonable week and one good week, then you'd have two bad ones. And when I kept checking the books it always seemed the same, one reasonable week, one good week and then two bad ones.*

An important element of maintaining these avoidance strategies was people's inability to admit their problems to others. This was manifested in a widespread refusal to seek advice. One woman talked of her attempts to get her husband to admit that they needed help:

> *I felt that we really needed help. I could feel that we were sinking really fast... he didn't like the idea. He was too proud, he wouldn't come with me*

It also enabled some people, in their desperation, to convince themselves that the advice they received from other people was not correct:

> *... He [advisor] told me to get out of the shop quickly because it was draining us, he told me to do a lot of things but [my partner] wouldn't do any of them.*

One couple were advised that the only way to even partly redeem their situation was to give up the business which had already taken up all of their financial resources and was still declining. In their certainty that they would be able to 'turn things around' they refused to even consider this option:

> *... I said... 'We're going to have to do something' and he said 'Well, the only other way is for you to get out, just go.' I says 'What do you*

> *mean?' He said 'Just walk away from the place'... I put down the phone
> and said 'No way we're doing that, we're not just leaving this. We've
> put too much in it.*

Some respondents were even too proud to accept advice which may have
helped them to continue trading;

> *They explained to me in great detail how to run the money better... and
> the advice was good, I felt, but it needed two of you to think it's good. I
> think my husband was too proud.*

There were a number of reasons for this refusal to recognise the gravity
of their situation and the unwillingness to accept help. First, people had
often refused to acknowledge their problems for so long that facing up
to them became a considerably more frightening prospect than it had
originally been – even with help and advice.

Second, pretending that the business problems they faced were simply
minor hiccups had almost become a *raison d'etre* for some respondents.
They had not only been lying to themselves about the extent of their difficulties, but often to their creditors, and to their families and friends as
well. Admitting that this was not, in fact, the case, would have taken an
emotional strength which the majority of people simply did not have.

Third, 'head in the sand' strategies often meant that, in addition to
ignoring existing problems, respondents had also generated new ones.
At this point, admitting the seriousness of their situation would also
involve accepting much of the responsibility for having exacerbated it.

Fourth, one of the most terrifying things about the run-up to small
business failure was respondents' inability to control events. One
described the point at which he felt he had lost control of his business
problems:

> *... we hit this spiral point... It really happened just like that. Once it
> started it just went.*

The resulting insecurity created by this lack of control made them unable
to open any aspect of their lives to scrutiny by a third party.

Having continued to trade for some time after they had recognised,
subconsciously at least, that their only real option was closure, respondents usually found that the decision to leave self-employment was taken
out of their hands. While the consolidators protected themselves from
the worst of the humiliation of business failure by attributing it to external causes, those who struggled on were unable to cope with the idea of
taking the final steps to close the business themselves. They isolated
themselves from the decision-making by waiting until something
happened which gave them no other choice but to cease trading.

Trigger events

Some people were able to identify actual trigger events which had made it impossible for them to continue trading. For others, the last straw was more symbolic. The decision to close was often less traumatic for people who experienced trigger events, because they could almost always absolve themselves of responsibility for the actual decision to close.

For example, one man had attempted to set up a Voluntary Arrangement with his creditors to pay off this debts. In reality, this repayment plan was unrealistic, yet the respondent was keen to try and carry on. When the proposed arrangement was rejected by his creditors, however, he had no choice other than bankruptcy. Another person was forced to close when a firm went into liquidation owing him a substantial amount of money. His employees had already been working without wages for a fortnight in anticipation of payment from this company. When the bank discovered that this late payment had not been forthcoming, they called in all of the money he owed. The only option open to him at this point was closure.

In yet another case, a couple finally recognised that they had run out of options when one of them was arrested for assaulting a bailiff. Despite having agreed a repayment plan with the brewery from whom they had bought their pub, two bailiffs arrived, during a private party, and began removing furniture from the bar. Knowing that it was illegal for the bailiffs to confiscate items which would prevent them from trading, they had tried to stop them. When the bailiffs refused to leave, one of the respondents lost his temper and hit one of the bailiffs. He was subsequently jailed for two weeks, leaving his partner, heavily pregnant, to run the business alone. The emotional trauma of this event simply '*took the fight out*' of them and they gave up trying. They explained:

> ... *we'd known for a while that we were on a loser. We knew we'd lost everything and it was only a matter of time before we got kicked out... You know if you have a bad time you always think 'Oh well, in six months time things will be better'... but when they took him to prison... that was the last straw because then they even took our dignity away.*

At this stage, they felt that events had moved beyond their control and they accepted that they were unable to cope. This finally enabled them to give up the fight to save the business.

In contrast, reacting to more symbolic triggers required more active involvement in the decision to close. They did, however, provide respondents with something to which they could attribute their decision-making.

For example, a young couple received an unexpected legacy which they thought would be enough to pay off their debts and allow them to treat themselves for the first time since they had started the business. However, when they sat down to work out the figures they discovered that, not only was the whole amount already committed to paying off their debts, but that it would still leave some unpaid. They recalled:

> *It was the morning that the legacy came through and the fact that we just sat down and worked out... it was a case of in one hand and straight out of the other. That's when we thought 'Well, what progress have we made? Absolutely nothing.'... I think that was the first time we'd ever discussed it... what the situation was.*

Others identified the 'last straw' which triggered their decision to close as particularly bad days in their business. While they may, in fact, have been little different from other days, they were recalled as significant turning points:

> *Then one day, well I... think I did thirty pounds in a day... sitting there from six in the morning until ten at night. And my oldest daughter... says 'Mum, you can't carry on like this'... so I just got in the car one Friday morning and I thought 'Right, I'm doing it'... and I just went in and just said 'I want to make myself bankrupt'.*

Giving up the struggle

A large proportion of the strugglers, however, carried on until they met the end of the road. These people only closed their businesses at the point at which they were simply too physically or emotionally exhausted to continue or when they felt there was nothing left for them to try. On the whole, they were very honest about the difficulties they experienced in thinking about business closure:

> *... you're sitting there, not wanting to tell them, 'Well yeah, you're right, we've made a great big booboo. We were wrong.' So you carry on for another twelve months pretending everything's okay... even, like, your parents and everybody, you want them to think, you know, how well you're doing and everything.*

When the strugglers did reach the point of considering closure it was usually because they were too exhausted to fulfil their business commitments. One explained that, one day, he simply felt:

> *I've had enough... I want to be out. If I thought I could save the business I would do... but I had enough... enough of trying to fight the banks, trying to keep it afloat and yet in my heart of hearts I couldn't see how any of us could do it.*

Eventually they had to make a decision to close the business for their own health and sanity:

> ... *I was finished but at least I wasn't being sucked down any further...* *that's the main thing. We're talking basic physical survival.*

These were, perhaps, the most negative circumstances in which to close a business. They had struggled on well beyond the point at which they recognised that they would be unable to reverse the decline and they could not see a way out. Having worn themselves out with the struggle to keep going, they simply succumbed to the inevitable.

Those who were still struggling

Respondents' motivations for continuing to struggle on with their business until they were faced with no alternative but closure is clearly illustrated by those who were still trading at the time of the research. The majority were embroiled in very similar situations to those described by people who had already closed their businesses. They did not anticipate any real improvements and were often waiting for the decision to be taken out of their hands.

Some demonstrated a clear acceptance that they were unlikely to be able to resolve their situations and were facing closure:

> *Initially it was an exercise to prove to myself whether I would have* *made it if I had gone the same way as some people did when I left* *school... I think I've proved to myself that... I was always going to be* *a worker, not going to be a businessman...*

They were often already suffering as a result of the struggle. One, who admitted that he had been fighting to keep his business going for the last six years, said:

> ... *it's there. It's not going to go away... so we're both sort of lumbered* *with this, getting up in the morning and going to bed at night. Nothing* *goes away itself.*

Yet somehow they still could not bring themselves to close the business down. Their inclination was still to hold on because of the personal investment they had made:

> *I... cry occasionally because starting the nursery five years ago, I see* *myself. It's me. It's what I've achieved over five years and to actually* *let it go, it's very difficult. But it's common sense at the end of the day.*

A key factor in these delaying tactics was a need for someone else to take responsibility for closing the business for them. Indeed, people in this situation were completely candid in their admission that this was their desired outcome:

> *I really wish they would make me bankrupt. I don't want to do it. I would like one of them to take me to court and make me bankrupt.*

Frequently, they were less scared of business failure than of having to endure the trauma of closing the business themselves:

> *I could get us off the hook, but my nature doesn't... allow me to do it. So, hence, what I am saying is, and I'll tell them to their face, 'Bankrupt me, I don't mind'.*

As a result, they were simply living with the daily anxiety that their businesses could collapse at any point. In the words of one, they were just waiting for *'everything to fall around our ears'*. Yet they still harboured the hope that things would either improve or that the decision would be taken out of their hands. Although they did not feel able to initiate closure themselves, a couple of people were desperately looking forward to the time when they could start to pick up the pieces. One said, wearily,

> *·I should love, at this moment in time, to be able to lock the door and walk away. But it's not that simple.*

When it finally occurs, small business failure is often the culmination of one of the most devastating periods of people's lives. Further, it brings with it a range of knock-on effects which combine to make the experience of small business failure extremely traumatic for everyone involved. In reality, these effects are intricately entwined and it is very difficult to understand them in isolation from their general context. However, for the purposes of this report we have separated them into two broad categories – those that affect people's financial circumstances and those which affect their personal lives. Chapter 4 looks at the financial impact of small business failure, drawing on the experiences of both groups of respondents: those who were struggling to continue to trade and those whose business had already failed. The personal impact of small business failure is the subject of Chapter 5.

Chapter 4

The Financial Impact of Small Business Failure

The financial impact of small business failure was for the most part unavoidable, devastating and long-term. The consequences were usually far more serious than most people had anticipated. Most of the people in this study whose businesses had failed had lost everything they had invested in setting the business up and keeping it running. On top of these losses, they had often also accrued substantial debts for which they retained responsibility even after the business had closed. Many were forced to face the harsh reality that ceasing to trade did not bring an end to the demands for money from their creditors. Moreover, having closed the business, most of them had lost their means of earning a living and paying off their debts.

In the midst of the slowly dawning reality of small business failure they had to make decisions about bankruptcy and insolvency. These decisions were crucial in shaping the nature and extent of their financial problems. In this chapter, we focus on the impact of small business failure on sole traders. The problems faced by legal partnerships tend to be far more complex.

BANKRUPTCY AND INSOLVENCY

The key financial impact of small business failure, for most respondents, related to their decision-making regarding bankruptcy. This was also the aspect of small business failure which they had, in their optimism, least considered. The 1986 Insolvency Act provides the legal framework for the bankruptcy law in England and Wales. Individuals facing insolvency can apply for a bankruptcy hearing through the High Court and most county courts, although they may be able to avoid bankruptcy by making an Individual Voluntary Arrangement with their creditors to pay off their debts.

Bankruptcy petitions

Some people, when faced with insurmountable financial difficulties, choose to make themselves insolvent because it offers a chance to lift their burden of debt and financial pressure. Bankruptcy affords the option of having their financial situation resolved by a third party. It also offers protection from creditors, and some groups of people – for example, those who do not own property, who are unemployed, or who have few material possessions – will lose far less from bankruptcy than from a Individual Voluntary Arrangement. Bankruptcy proceedings can be initiated against debtors by one or more of their creditors, although over half of all bankruptcy petitions each year are made by the debtors themselves.

The various stages of bankruptcy are supervised by the courts, who also act as mediators, between the parties involved. Once bankruptcy proceedings have begun, Official Receivers become involved in the case. It is their responsibility to:

- investigate the affairs of the bankrupt and report to the court, where necessary;
- report to the court when the bankrupt applies to be discharged;
- attend hearings and serve notices associated with the case;
- ensure that the bankrupt supplies a statement of affairs; and
- act as an Interim Receiver.

An Interim Receiver is appointed to protect the bankrupt's estate during the time between the petition for bankruptcy and the discharge of the bankruptcy order. The Interim Receiver takes responsibility for:

- overseeing or disposing of perishable goods;
- disposing of goods of diminishing value;
- avoiding the incurring of any additional expenditure after the petition;
- protecting the bankrupt's estate from creditors; and
- calling a creditors' meeting to appoint a Trustee to administer the estate if there are sufficient assets.

Once an individual is judged as bankrupt by the courts, s/he is subject to a number of restrictions. The main consequences of being an undischarged bankrupt are as follows:

- their bankruptcy can be advertised in the local paper or in the *London Gazette* – a publication which is consulted by Credit Reference agencies;

- they are unable to own property (except in some special circumstances, see below) and must hand over all property, records, leases, bank books, life policies, pensions and credit cards;
- they are unable to hold public office or be director of a company without leave of court;
- they cannot obtain credit over £250 without declaring their status as a bankrupt;
- they must notify the Trustee or Official Receiver within 21 days of all property received or increases in income;
- if businesses continue to trade, they must trade in the same name; and
- bank and building society accounts are frozen as soon as notice of the bankruptcy order is received; their continued use is at the bank's discretion after consultation with the Official Receivers/Trustee.

Discharge from bankruptcy is automatic unless a person has been bankrupt before during the previous 15 years, or the bankruptcy is a criminal case. Discharge takes place after two or three years, depending on the circumstances of the case. After discharge the bankrupt is released from all debts except fraudulent or secured debts, fines, damages for negligence, maintenance and various other criminal obligations.

Individual Voluntary Arrangements

The Individual Voluntary Arrangement was introduced by the 1986 Insolvency Act, as an alternative to bankruptcy. Individual Voluntary Arrangements, as opposed to bankruptcy, are negotiated where the debtor has assets available to be distributed. Individual Voluntary Arrangements normally require around £10,000 of available assets in order to succeed. While income is not, strictly speaking, considered a negotiable asset for an Individual Voluntary Arrangement, in practice Individual Voluntary Arrangements can be set up, based on the repayment of at least part of a debt from future income.

Under an Individual Voluntary Arrangement, debtors can avoid bankruptcy by reaching a 'commercial arrangement' with their creditors in order to discharge their debts. In some circumstances, Individual Voluntary Arrangements are considered to be preferable to bankruptcy, by both creditors and debtors, because they assure creditors of debt recovery and the debtor avoids the consequences of bankruptcy. Individual Voluntary Arrangements are also much less formal and expensive. However, they are not available to partnerships – each member of a partnership must negotiate a separate Arrangement with creditors.

Individual Voluntary Arrangements can be initiated in three sets of circumstances:

- by the debtor when s/he sees s/he is insolvent;
- when s/he is referred on a debtor's petition; and
- when the bankrupt's Trustee considers it to be of benefit to the creditors.

They are normally initiated by the debtor, who approaches an Insolvency Practitioner for advice.

Individual Voluntary Arrangements enable debtors to avoid bankruptcy and its associated stigma. Debtors who set up Individual Voluntary Arrangements are also relieved of the legal restrictions which are placed on people who are bankrupt. Any workable proposal for repaying debts can be submitted for negotiation and payment plans can, therefore, be quite flexible. Perhaps most importantly, where a debtor's business is viable, Individual Voluntary Arrangements allow the business to survive, providing debtors with the opportunity to trade out of trouble or sell the business as a going concern.

Individual Voluntary Arrangements also offer a number of advantages for creditors. They are a relatively uncomplicated and flexible method of reasonably assured debt recovery. Creditors can apply to have a bankruptcy petition enforced as soon as a debtor defaults on the Arrangement. They also ensure that creditors do not suffer financially, giving them a continued right to claim 17.5 per cent VAT bad debt relief, just as they would if the debtor was to go bankrupt. Under Individual Voluntary Arrangements creditors also have the right to claim interest on all their debtors' accounts.

However, Individual Voluntary Arrangements also have their drawbacks. Should a debtor default on an Individual Voluntary Arrangement, creditors have no power to enforce it and their only option is to return to court to present a bankruptcy petition. Re-negotiations of Arrangements following changes of circumstances are costly in both time and fees for Insolvency Practitioners. Businesses which continue to trade require monitoring by Insolvency Practitioners, which is also costly. Further the Arrangement can also be undermined by Government Departments – Inland Revenue, Customs and Excise – who may refuse to be involved, as they are considered priority creditors in bankruptcy.

THE RUN-UP TO BUSINESS FAILURE

The desperate financial straits of people experiencing business problems were clearly illustrated by the respondents who were still trading at the time of this study. Although most of them had accepted that closure was imminent, they were continuing to juggle with their finances to try to stave off the implications of their debts. Some had already suffered severe financial losses. All of those who were still trading had substantial debts covering both business and personal expenses. These were for sums ranging from £5,000 to £72,500 and included debts with suppliers and subcontractors; rent for trading premises; council tax and the local business rate; mortgages for domestic property; personal credit cards and domestic utility bills.

Evidence suggests that people had first of all fallen behind with payments relating to their business, usually to suppliers, or with their rent or business rate. Personal credit card bills were the next to get out of hand as these were used to generate short-term cash for the business. This was quickly followed by mortgage arrears as more personal resources were redirected towards the business as a short-term, stabilising measure. However, most continued to experience serious financial difficulties as they juggled with their bills. After this, council tax and utility bills went unpaid as part of a desperate juggling act to try to make ends meet. For some people, this juggling act had gone on for so long that they simply did not know which way to turn. One described his situation:

> ... what I've done is I've actually, literally, burnt all my boats to keep my head above water...I have nothing left.

Another portrayed the desperation of his circumstances even more eloquently:

> Everybody is like a butcher around me and I am like a sheep in the hands of the butchers. They like to cut me, they all want to eat the meat.

At the time of this study one respondent had had his telephone cut off for non-payment of bills. Losing this means of communication with other family members, who were very geographically dispersed, was a source of great concern but had been unavoidable. The respondent faced little prospect of raising the money required for re-connection. Another had had to have a pre-payment electricity meter installed because he had built up substantial arrears.

> I mean, it's had a knock-on effect now. I mean we're trying to make agreements to pay people but, like the electricity, unfortunately that's gone by the wayside and some time over the next week or fortnight they want two hundred and forty quid off me, and I haven't got it so we're having to have a card meter fitted. You know, it's just one of those things, there's no point trying to wriggle out of it any more...

Although he had offered a payment of £100 to the electricity company to avoid having the meter fitted, his long-standing debts meant that he was considered too unreliable for the offer to be accepted. This was the only way the electricity company would agree to continue his supply and, with a very young baby in the family, he could not risk being cut off.

Yet another person had had personal possessions impounded by bailiffs for non-payment of council tax.

> ... *the bailiffs have actually already been and collected certain items out of the house already... microwave, radio, lawnmower and part of my working equipment which they actually returned... so we had to give them fifty quid.*

Having fallen behind with his council tax repayments again, he faced a further visit from the bailiffs. His main concern was that he had few possessions left which could be appropriated:

> *I rang them up and said 'Look, you sent me this letter, you reckon the bailiff's coming round today... I'm paying you off the best means I can, you've been in and taken stuff out of my house, there isn't anything else left for you to take, unless you start taking necessity items like fridges and washing machines...'*

With no other means to make good his liability for the debt, however, he was very uncertain as to whether he could hold off the bailiffs any longer.

A particularly infuriating situation faced by a few people was a continued liability for consumer goods that had recently been bought on hire purchase, even after the items had been repossessed. This happened to one man who had been unable to maintain the hire purchase payments on a car he had bought.

> *I had a car which was repossessed because I couldn't keep up the repayments... so what happened then is they took the car back and they sold it for obviously a lot less than it was worth. So then I got lumbered with the balance of what I owed them and what they sold it for. So now I've got another bill.*

Continuing liability for this debt, even after he had lost possession of the car, was something which he found it very difficult to deal with, particularly as he badly needed the money to pay off other debts.

Most of the people who were still trading at the time of the research faced continuing financial problems, and were juggling with their income and expenditure to try and keep their heads above water. One young man who had made a firm commitment to continue trading, and was confident in his ability to 'trade out of trouble', also recognised the short-termism of his approach to debt management. He had been paying off his smaller debts and ignoring a large tax liability although he knew that the tax bill ought to be his priority. He explained:

> ... *we don't want to open that sort of bees nest yet, when we're sort of looking at everything else. Whereas, really, it is the highest priority, because everything else is so much easier to cope with we're dealing with that first which is wrong, we know, but if we can get shot of that we can concentrate on the tax.*

Although dealing with the smaller debts, over which he had more control, gave him the confidence he needed to continue trading, he was aware of the threat that his unpaid tax demand presented. A number of other respondents had adopted short-term strategies such as this, to keep their business going. However, most recognised that, without an upturn in their fortunes, they were unlikely to avoid closure and, for some, bankruptcy. One man, who had already avoided bankruptcy once by setting up a Individual Voluntary Arrangement to pay off debts to his main creditors, was being 'leant on' by new creditors, over debts he had accrued directly as a result of ring-fencing the money needed to fulfil this arrangement. He explained:

> *I'm still paying it, you know, I'm still able to pay it. It is getting more difficult... we get letters from other people now, different companies... after a while because things weren't improving... it just seems it's built up and up again and we're nearly to the same situation as we were before I took out the [Individual] Voluntary Arrangement.*

Because Individual Voluntary Arrangements take a great deal of both time and money to alter, the respondent's new creditors could not be incorporated into it. As a result, he was stuck in a vicious circle. The creditors who were not part of the Individual Voluntary Arrangement had no incentive not to keep pressing him for payment and threatening him with legal action. As a result, he felt that he should prioritise these debts in order to 'buy some time'. Yet defaulting payment on his Individual Voluntary Arrangement meant that his creditors could automatically enforce a bankruptcy petition against him.

Several other people had incurred mortgage arrears in an attempt to keep their businesses going and had received possession orders on their homes. The threat of possession held a particularly deep fear and, while some had lost their homes, others were prepared to go to great lengths to avoid it. One had cashed in an endowment policy which would, seven years later, have been worth a substantial amount of money, to cover debts of only a few thousand.

> *I have had problems before but I cashed in an endowment on this [house] to get from under them [the building society] and that was the biggest problem of my life because I only had another seven years to run on that endowment which would have produced for me £70-£80 thousand. I had no choice, it was either that or go under.*

Cashing in the endowment early meant forfeiting money which would have offered a long-term solution to his financial problems and provided financial security during his retirement. Perhaps worse than this was the fact that cashing in the endowment had proved to be only a short-term solution to his problems. By the time of interview, this respondent had accrued further mortgage arrears and was, again, being threatened with possession. He explained:

> *I can show you a letter in there, that arrived two days ago, that says... if I can't get up to bring the arrears into line... then they will take legal action.*

At this point, he had nothing left to offer the building society to stave off his worst fears. Without the heart to contact them, he was simply waiting to see what would happen.

Many other people lived in a state of constant anxiety that their homes would be possessed, as they knew they had no means of paying off their rising mortgage arrears. One ruefully remarked:

> *I have nothing left, this isn't my house really now, it belongs to a building society and they, right at this moment, are threatening me, as well, that this could be gone by the end of the year.*

Another, a young mother desperately trying to keep both her business and her family together against mounting financial pressure and family tension, explained:

> *I live in fear that somebody can come in and... say no, we want this... sold. The person at the moment is very sympathetic and is helping us... but somebody else can come and take over and, I don't know if it's policy for the bank to be sympathetic at the start, or will they just come and say 'We've had enough, we want our money back, we don't care how you do it'? So that's the fear I live in...*

This woman was practically at the end of her tether at the time of interview. She was so worn down by the constant threat of losing her home that she had decided to try to sell her business.

One man, despite having set up a repayment plan with his bank, had had to sell his home after they threatened to possess if he did not pay off his mortgage arrears in full.

They were saying that I wasn't getting the money back quick enough. So, in the end, three years ago, what I did, I sold the house, bought a smaller one and with the difference between the two I cleared most of the debt off.

He found it a huge wrench to sell the home that he and his wife and shared for almost 30 years but knew that he had little choice. If his home had been possessed there would have been little, if any, money left after his debts had been repaid and, consequently, he would have been unable to buy another property.

Well, I mean none of us wanted to leave, really... we'd got very good neighbours up the road... but it was the fact that we needed the cash, you know and, as I say, we were more or less forced into it by the bank.

Yet he found that losing the family 'base' had a big impact on his family life. Both of his children continued their social lives in the area in which they'd used to live and, as a result, spent much less time at home.

I mean, my lad he'll go out of a weekend, and he very rarely comes home of a Saturday night because he stays with his friends... because he won't drink and drive...

He and his wife had also found it difficult establishing roots in a new area:

... because this is a new estate that we've gone onto, and with us both being out at work all day, you only see people of a weekend and, you know, you're slow to make friends...

They had developed few social networks in their new area and they too, found, that their social life was largely restricted to their old neighbourhood. As a result, they rarely went out, as travelling back to where they used to live was expensive. They found this very isolating.

Most of the respondents who were still trading at the time of interview were in the process of trying to judge whether they had more to lose by struggling on or by quitting. Most still felt that they had made too much of a personal investment in the business to close it down themselves. Yet they knew that they would never be able to make enough money to survive in the long term. This was often exacerbated by the fact that the longer they stayed open, the more debts they accrued and the more money they needed to earn to finance their growing range of debts. This vicious circle put them under huge financial pressure and resulted in constant worry and anxiety. One explained:

> *You've got to keep going to survive. But you want to stop and you can't, there's always something in the way, you've got to do something, to pay for something...*

Another presented a more chilling image of what his life had become:

> *It's like a cancer, I mean it's like having... it's difficult not to interfere with my everyday work... constantly I'm updating my statements and updating my cashflow to see where I'm going to be in four weeks time or whatever, depending on what monies I think are coming in. So, it's a cancer, it's there all the time. It never leaves me. I can't have a day off and not think about it.*

Many of these people were desperately awaiting the time when it somehow became clear to them that they could not continue. Further, as we saw in Chapter 3, many were waiting for a third party to put an end to their problems for them. One said:

> *I still come back to thinking, 'I could get rid of it all, I could get us off the hook' but my nature doesn't allow me to do it so, hence... I say to them, 'Bankrupt me, I don't mind'. I'm not going to lose, I'm going to end up much better for it afterwards.*

Another said:

> *Well, the way I feel... I'm looking forward to the fact that I'm going to be forced to pack up. I've come to the point now where I feel tired. It's a burden to get up in the morning and go out to work.*

AFTER SMALL BUSINESS FAILURE

The combination of delayed or unwise reactions to the situation, ineffectiveness in dealing with problems and mixing business and personal finances, meant that most people whose businesses had failed had accrued substantial debts and losses.

Very few people had left self-employment without debts – most had lost amounts ranging from £500 to £130,000. Again, these covered a range of personal and business liabilities. Of 27 respondents who had ceased to trade, eight had already lost their homes, and a further nine were threatened with possession. Two respondents were homeless at the time of the research; another couple with a very young baby had been officially categorised as homeless, and were housed by their local authority.

None of the people who had ceased to trade were really prepared for the full financial impact of closing their business. Having already lost everything they had put into the business and, in some cases, their homes and personal possessions as well, they were devastated to find that they still owed money.

> *All the stock I'd got, I had £6–7,000 worth of stock, we agreed that's what I owed him [landlord] for my lease, because I gave my lease up early... I never came out with a penny. Fifteen thousand in and come out with nothing. So we're just paying off now what we can afford. It's a struggle... I've got two [years] left of the [council tax] and there's the [building society] for ten years.*

Only a couple of people had managed to close their businesses without substantial debts. One had maintained a very prudent attitude towards credit and borrowing, even during the successful years of his business. He joked ruefully:

> *Must be the only company that's ever gone bankrupt without owing the bank a penny!*

Another's debts were inherited by the family business he had been running and he carried no liability for them after he ceased to run the business. Positive choice entrants and some entrepreneurs were usually the most fortunate in this respect, in that they could sell off elements of their business to recoup some of their losses. One auctioned his specialist engineering equipment, another sold his client base. This way, they managed to regain at least some of their initial outlay and clear most of their debts.

People whose businesses had high fixed costs, usually reluctant recruits, constrained choice entrants and some of the entrepreneurs, who ran shops, pubs and so on, were in the worst position. Although, in theory, they should have been able to recover at least some of their fixed costs by selling the business as a going concern, they often had difficulty finding buyers, particularly during the recession. In addition, they were often behind on the payments for these fixed costs – rent, leases, equipment and so on, and had little to gain, even had they been able to sell.

Of the respondents who had substantial debts when they ceased to trade, just under half went bankrupt; the rest set up Individual Voluntary Arrangements or informal agreements with their creditors to pay off their debts. Several of those who, in the event, went bankrupt had hoped to avoid doing so, by setting up Individual Voluntary Arrangements. But this strategy had been unsuccessful. One of them, for example, was simply not in a position to meet the accountants' fees:

> *... we went into that [Individual Voluntary Arrangement] but, again, they wanted thousands off us to make a voluntary arrangement... they all wanted money, everybody wanted money.*

Others, however, paid Insolvency Practitioners to propose a Voluntary Agreement only to find that they were not accepted by all their creditors. One explained:

> *... we went through all the rigmarole of agreeing payment structure plans for all the people that were owed money, and everybody accepted it except one... and they made me bankrupt. So for the one company making me bankrupt for £8,000, nobody got paid.*

Another respondent had suffered because priority debtors, such as the Inland Revenue and Customs and Excise, can refuse to accept these agreements. He desperately wanted the business to continue trading and was relying on a Voluntary Agreement to allow him to clear his debts without putting the business in jeopardy. Despite a long and unblemished trading record, medical evidence stating that his VAT and Inland Revenue debts had accrued during a period in which he had been too ill to properly administer the business and clear evidence that the business was still profitable, his Voluntary Agreement was refused by Customs and Excise:

> *... the VAT told them... that there was no way they wanted me in business again, that they weren't willing to support any administration order to method of payment. They wanted me out of business totally...*

With their creditors not willing to support an Individual Voluntary Arrangement, these respondents had no option but bankruptcy.

Perceptions of bankruptcy

People's perceptions of bankruptcy were crucial to the financial impact of small business failure in two respects. First, because bankruptcy was so widely viewed as 'admitting defeat'. Consequently, most shied away from the whole idea, refusing even to consider it until their circumstances became really desperate. Second, because by the time many people accepted the need to consider bankruptcy their financial problems had worsened to such a degree that it was often their only option. Even then, however, many found it very difficult to accept in practice. One couple explained:

It's one of those things that happen to other people, things you read about. It's not going to happen to you.

For the majority of people in the study, bankruptcy was the ultimate admission of failure. One said:

Obviously I tried to keep going because under the insolvency laws... there's this awful stigma... there's a stigma of failure everywhere.

These perceptions were usually fuelled by a lack of knowledge about bankruptcy procedures. Most people believed that 'going bankrupt' involved a court appearance at which they would be required to give evidence and defend their position.

It's worrying because if you've never had trouble in your life and you're faced with a court appearance, it was frightening.

In essence, they viewed bankruptcy hearings as a judgement on their culpability and their right to be discharged of the responsibility for their debts. In reality, however, this is not the case. Bankruptcy hearings are held in Chambers, before a District Judge, rather than in open court. This means that the proceedings are relatively informal, and conducted in an office type room with all the parties involved sitting around a table. People who had received advice about bankruptcy and, therefore, had a clearer idea of what was involved found the decision easier to make because this knowledge reduced their fear of the unknown. One person who had received advice from a specialist business debt counselling service said:

... basically what she did, she told me more about bankruptcy and she told me what the procedures were like at that time... so she told me what was really... going on at that time concerning bankruptcy, how they were reacting... just sort of like put a few fears at rest, you know.

Experiences of bankruptcy

Misconceptions about bankruptcy proceedings meant that people's expectations were usually far worse than their actual experiences of going bankrupt. In fact, most people had found the procedure far simpler and more business-like than they had expected. One said:

Well, we decided on the Sunday afternoon... and then the following morning we got in the car and went to Sheffield and we just filled this

*form in and he took us to this other office where the magistrate was
and said 'Right, that's it, you're bankrupt now'.*

One couple likened the procedure to visiting a bank:

F: *It was like a bank, you go up to the girl and you say 'Here's the
papers, we've filled them out'. You had to list everything you
owed... It's cheaper doing it as a couple than two separate people
and you just fill it all in, everything you owe and then she takes
that...*

M: *She went round to some judge or something and he signed it and
then come back and she says 'That's it'... I think we were only
there two hours.*

F: *She just wanted to know quickly what happened, we told her... a
short thing, a few sentences... and that was it, and then you get
forms telling you what you can and can't do... it was dead simple.*

Many people were also surprised to find that bankruptcy proceedings
were not concerned with apportioning blame. One man was very taken
aback at the civility he had encountered over a procedure in which he
felt his guilt would heavily implicated.

*He was most pleasant... when I came to go, the registrar actually got
up and opened the door and he said, 'I'm very sorry, Mr Atkins, that's
all I could do'...*

In fact, most found court officials and official receivers pleasant to deal
with and, in some cases, openly sympathetic. One described the sensi-
tivity a judge had shown her husband when he was clinically depressed
over his business failure.

*... he got himself into such as state about facing anybody, but he had to
go... and the judge had him go into the chambers and he said, 'It's
nothing to be ashamed of', he said, 'You were just very unfortunate
when you bought the business and I'm hearing this every day of the
week' and he was really understanding.*

In fact, for a few people, the proceedings were so quick and easy that
they found it something of an anti-climax, particularly after everything
they had put themselves through to try to avoid it.

*When we walked out of the place, the woman said 'That's it, all done
now'. We walked out and I thought, 'I can't believe it'. We were expecting to have to go and sit in court, people question you and all sorts.*

They felt they would have valued the opportunity to state their case in full and, as they viewed it, be publicly relieved of blame. Yet the detailed facts of their case appeared to be of little interest.

Negative experiences of bankruptcy

Although most people in the study who had been made bankrupt had found it easier and less traumatic than they had anticipated, a few had still found it very unpleasant. Often this was related to their perception of bankruptcy as a public admission of guilt. Some people, particularly those who had had little opportunity to discuss their problems prior to bankruptcy, found it deeply distressing to talk about their circumstances with others.

> *I had to attend court... and I broke down, I started crying. The build-up of various things...*

Others found the whole process of attending court and recounting debts a very distasteful experience. This was particularly the case for older people, who had never expected to have to account for themselves in any kind of court:

> *... we went out to the court...it was a very traumatic experience. Neither of us had ever been in a court before. You know, I'm forty-seven and I've never been in a court, not where it's been me that's sat there anyway.*

In addition, a few people who had not received any advice or counselling were haunted by the feeling that they had made a mistake in filing for bankruptcy. Sometimes this was because they were concerned that they had 'given in' too easily and ignored other options which would have allowed them to continue to trade and pay off their debts.

However, a small group of people who had been forced into bankruptcy by their creditors were extremely bitter about their experiences. One person, in particular, noted the bitter irony of his situation after having his Individual Voluntary Arrangement rejected:

> *It was the most unbelievable feeling that you can walk out of the bankruptcy court and think, 'Well, all those people have been kicking up a fuss about getting money and they're not going to get anything, and it's their own silly fault...'*

Despite recognising this irony, people who had been made bankrupt by their creditors found it much harder to cope with than those who had chosen to do so themselves. One man said:

> *Subsequently, of course, personally it has caused me a lot more anguish and, like I say I'm still suffering from it.*

THE IMPACT OF BANKRUPTCY

As undischarged bankrupts, respondents faced a number of constraints on their lives and activities. The legal restrictions imposed on undischarged bankrupts mean that, among other things they:

- they cannot own property and must hand over assets such as life insurance policies and pensions;
- can operate bank or building society accounts only at the discretion of their bank;
- must hand over credit cards and are unable to obtain credit over £250 without declaring their status as a bankrupt.

In practice, these conditions affected people's lives in a number of ways.

Housing

Several of the people in our study had already had their homes possessed, prior to bankruptcy, as a result of mortgage arrears. However, undischarged bankrupts must, in most cases, hand over any property they own which is then sold to cover their debts. Consequently, even those who had continued to pay their mortgage throughout their business problems still found themselves unable to retain their house after their business had failed. For most people, this was the most traumatic impact of bankruptcy, from which the whole family suffered. One was unable to put the stress of his family's experience into words:

> *Well, she was very sad.. I can't really describe it in words. It was just a horrible feeling really...*

On top of the trauma of losing a family home, some people were extremely frustrated to lose their homes only for them to stand empty awaiting a buyer.

> *[We] went bankrupt first and then [lost] the house about three of four months after... it was stood empty for about a year because we offered*

> *to live in it... but pay them some rent money. We offered that, and then we're still in it... at least keep the place warm, because it was an old place. They wouldn't have it, they wouldn't listen [they said] OUT!!!*

People who had lost their homes as a result of bankruptcy faced a whole new set of problems in finding new accommodation. Very few had dependent children at the time and were not, therefore, considered a priority for either local authority or housing association properties. Unable to own property and with restrictions on their access to credit as undischarged bankrupts, they were forced into the rented sector, either for the first time in their lives or the first time since their youth. Most had no other option than to rent from private landlords, whose properties were frequently expensive and in poor condition. Their chances of finding decent, affordable and good quality properties to rent were often greatly reduced by the fact that very few had managed to find new employment by the time they were seeking housing.

Some had to accept accommodation which was in poor condition and unsuitable for their family's needs. One was forced to move his entire family, including three young children, into one room in a house belonging to friends while they were on the waiting list for a housing association property. He recounted:

> *That was a very difficult situation, there was a lot of tension in the family, a lot of tension because we basically had to live in one room. You know, for a while, for about four months. And so we had a young baby as well. And there was no gas at the place we were staying, it was just electric so we had to use electric heaters. But still the place was absolutely freezing and all of us came down with colds and the poor baby kept on having colds week after week, it was a terrible situation.*

Fearful of imposing on their friends' lifestyle, they spent most of their time cooped up in their room. Their four-month stay included the Christmas period, during which the whole family was cold and unwell. Fortunately, their housing association property, when it became available, was considerably more comfortable and spacious.

Others, unable to provide the financial references required by letting agencies, were forced to rent from private individuals. These arrangements were sometimes less secure. One couple moved into a rented property to find out, only a few weeks later, that their landlord was himself in serious financial difficulty. They remembered with some amusement:

> *... we had the sheriff's office, we had bailiffs, we had all sorts looking for him. He'd got behind with his mortgage payments. So we had to move out of that, we was in that just over a year and they repossessed it.*

They also often found it difficult to find private landlords who would accept tenants who were receiving Housing Benefit. One, looking for somewhere to move with her daughter and very elderly mother, explained:

> *Yes, he wanted business people because he'd had trouble with benefits... I was a week trying to persuade [the landlord] that we could afford it, because he was worried we wouldn't.*

Her landlord also turned out to be less than scrupulous and was, at the time of the interview, trying to demand that she pay him additional rent on top of the Housing Benefit payment he was receiving, on her behalf, from the local authority. She said:

> *At the moment I'm having a bit of trouble with him... they [Housing Benefit] pay him £235.40 every four weeks but he's wanting us to make it up to £300 a month... I got onto the Citizen's Advice Bureau, they got onto the benefits office... and they said... [He] should know all about it because he's got enough properties and he's dealt with us before. So I think he's trying it on.*

Although she was planning to tackle him about it, she was fearful of causing too much trouble in case her landlord refused to renew her lease at the end of her tenancy agreement:

> *I don't want to be too much trouble because it's only a year's tenancy and really I want to stick here now, you know, I don't want to be moving again, apart from anything else it's the turmoil for my mother. When we moved here... she cried when she saw this place.*

In general, however, although they were clearly affected by the loss of their homes, this was not something they attributed specifically to bankruptcy. The majority, aware that the situation had arisen as a result of their business debts, tended to perceive the loss of their home as a result of being in debt, rather than being bankrupt.

The restrictions on undischarged bankrupts' rights to own property are slightly more flexible in some circumstances. A bankrupt's spouse is entitled to a 'grace' period of one year during which s/he can continue to occupy the property although they may be required to sell the property after that period, in order to meet creditors' interests. In addition, people with dependent children are given the same period of grace, in order to minimise the effects of bankruptcy.

Decisions about whether or not an undischarged bankrupt will be required to sell a property after the grace period has expired are made after consideration of a number of factors. These include the interests of creditors, the extent to which spouses are perceived to have contributed to the bankruptcy, and the needs, financial and otherwise, of the spouse and any children. This period of grace and the subsequent wait to discover whether or not they will be required to leave their home was an extremely unsettling time. A few people were still waiting to find out whether or not they would lose their homes at the time of the research. One said:

> ... we haven't heard a thing off them in over three years now... it's still unresolved... it's just lying dormant at the moment.

An even more unsettling situation evolved where negative equity on a property meant that it was not worth selling, because it would not raise any money. Often people in this situation did not fully understand why they had not had to sell their home or how likely it was that they would be required to do so in the future. This group, in particular, felt like 'hostages to fortune' as they waited to see whether an upturn in the housing market would mean that they had to leave their homes. These circumstances were extremely frustrating for people who felt they were forced to simply stand on the sidelines while other people decided their fate.

Financial restrictions

Respondents were also affected by legal restrictions on their finances as undischarged bankrupts. Often this was the first time in their adult lives that their financial activities had been constrained. For some of the entrepreneurs, losing their access to credit was the worst possible thing that could happen. One man, who had previously been a speculative property developer, felt that he would be unable to resume these activities, even after his bankruptcy was discharged.

> This is the biggest thing, you see... the only stigma is that you cannot go out and borrow money ever again. It's not three years later, you don't get a ticket that suddenly says you can borrow money again, that thing comes up on those buttons on that computer all the time. ' This man was a bankrupt, made bankrupt'.

In fact, bankruptcy is time-limited and, in most circumstances, discharge is automatic after three years.

The less intrepid respondents, in particular some of the reluctant recruits and constrained choice entrants, were much less affected by the constraints. In fact, the experience of having owed so much money meant that some were quite comforted by the restrictions on their access to credit. The experience of substantial debt and financial difficulty close behind them, they were reassured by the fact that they were 'safe' from building up any more debt. One remarked:

> *Ralph had credit cards, but I don't think we'd bother with that again....*
> *We both said, 'We are better off now than what we have been, no more*
> *credit or anything'.*

They often expressed a fear of borrowing in the light of recent experiences:

> *No, we're not bothered about the credit, because we'd never have*
> *anything again unless we paid for it.*

However, whatever their feelings about more general constraints, most were inconvenienced by them in practice. In particular, they were hampered by the absence of a current account and cheque book which constrained even their most basic financial needs. For example, one respondent had to negotiate with her bank to allow her to open a savings account simply so that she could pay in her Housing Benefit cheque.

> *Paula went and explained to them and they've allowed her to have a*
> *savings account, but the only reason was so we could pay the rent. So*
> *we could pay the rent cheque in because we had no way of paying it.*

However, she was not allowed any other banking facilities.

Others discovered that the absence of a cheque book or bank account from which to pay direct debits or standing orders made their financial transactions more costly. One couple commented:

> M: *It's a lot cheaper if you can write a cheque isn't it, it's easier.*
> F: *Yeah, if you've got to send it. Sending postal orders was costing us*
> *a blooming fortune.*

Others found that a few companies, geared up to more automated payment systems, were unhappy dealing with cash payments or postal orders. One said:

> *Some people, actually the car insurance, they were getting bit upset*
> *because we were sending them postal orders through.*

One couple, having been in arrears with their electricity bill in the past, found that the electricity company required a substantial deposit from them before they would agree to reconnect their supply. Unable to afford the deposit and with no access to borrowing facilities, they were forced to agree to having a card meter installed.

> *You see, people want you to pay direct debit and we can't. We had to have a card meter put in, they wouldn't let us have an account unless we put a couple of hundred pounds up front which we didn't have, so we couldn't do that. So we had to have a card meter.*

However, despite initial difficulties in dealing with these constraints, in the longer term most respondents managed to adapt, often without too much difficulty. For some, this involved relying on other people who had access to banking facilities to write them cheques. Others were able to alter their lifestyles to take account of these constraints, and managed to continue their lives with relatively little disruption. In fact, those with few dependents found that bankruptcy offered them a freedom and a financial security that self-employment could not provide. One explained:

> *I'm easier in my mind now, because I know exactly what's coming in. Although it's only a smattering, at least I know exactly what's coming in so that I can live appropriately.*

Another also felt relatively positive about his current situation:

> *Like I say, I've always been a loner. So I haven't been one for going out every night, I'm used to staying in. So in that respect it's had no consequence on me at all. In fact, I'm actually, I know it sounds ironic, but I'm actually better off, because I haven't got the worry. So emotionally I'm better off and financially I can actually save around £5 a week out of what I'm getting.*

However, a few were profoundly depressed by the prospect of up to five years of financial restrictions and limited access to money. In particular, the fact that undischarged bankrupts are unable to receive any money or property took away their hope that things might improve. While one remarked quite flippantly, *'There's no point in winning the lottery now!'* another said, flatly:

> *I've got to wait three years now as from 14th March. I can go to work, I think they allow you a certain amount of money to live on but, I mean, I can't receive anything else... Like if anybody left me anything in a will or anything, that would automatically go to the receiver. Anything like that, so I can't foresee anything for the next three years...*

Guilt and stigma

In addition to the practical effects of bankruptcy, some respondents felt an acute guilt over being 'a bankrupt'. Some were plagued with guilt at not paying off their debts and many expressed strong ethical concerns about being able to walk away too easily from a mess that they felt was of their own making.

> *... everybody... says that, under the circumstances, bankruptcy was going to be the best avenue for me to clear the debt out. The fact that morally I wanted to pay it, which I still feel very guilty about. The fact that yes, I did incur it... subconsciously the debt is still there... so morally I still feel guilty about owing some money and the fact that they have taken away the only means I had of paying them back...*

Another also felt a continued responsibility for closing the business before making good their debts:

> *I mean, okay, it's to relieve you of some of your debts but it doesn't make you feel any better that you can't pay all of these people back. They just think that you couldn't care less but I could. I didn't like owing people all over the place. It's a terrible thing...*

Others felt a more general stigma over being declared bankrupt. One perceived bankruptcy as a reflection on her ability to manage all aspects of her life:

> *It's the stigma, isn't it, attached to it as well, going bankrupt... You know, one minute you're doing alright, you've got your own business and the next minute you've lost everything. Sort of, something wonderful about owning your own business and doing well and then when it all goes against you... it's terrible.*

Another felt that bankruptcy implied a weakness in him and an unwillingness to carry on struggling, even for something which was important to him. To him, bankruptcy signalled his failure to fight as much as his failure to run a business.

> *I couldn't tell anyone I was going bankrupt because I couldn't bring myself to do it... I still thought I should fight on.*

One believed the stigma of bankruptcy would throw his entire professional ability into question, saying:

> '*... with my record now, as a bankrupt... you're finished, at my age.*'

Having tried self-employment and failed, this man believed he would never find a job again.

Relief and uncertainty

Clearly, where bankruptcy represented an end to most of their worries and demands from creditors, bankruptcy came as something of a relief. Some people's debts were so serious by the time they closed their businesses that bankruptcy was an inevitable next step. They viewed it as the only way to finally close the door and put the episode behind them. This was particularly the case for people who had continued to face demands from their creditors even after their businesses had closed.

Consequently, the majority of people who went bankrupt ultimately found it a huge relief, representing the end of a very traumatic phase of their lives and signalling a new start. One couple, when asked how they had felt after they had been declared bankrupt, said:

> F: *Oh, it was lovely. It was like a great big weight had been lifted off.*
> M: *It was like somebody just lifting it off your chest.*

They were not cavalier in their attitude to bankruptcy, they had simply been at the end of their tether and were unable to see any other way forward. Others were more guarded in their expressions of relief. One said, with exhaustion:

> *I'm glad I'm out of it now, the way it's been... Not to have the headache of juggling money, robbing Peter to pay Paul, it got like a daily basis...*

However, they certainly did not view it as an easy option.

> *I don't think anybody should take going bankrupt lightly. You shouldn't do it because you think you're going to escape from paying all these people off.*

> *... it were like a weight off my shoulders, you know, but I don't think I'd got away with it, I don't think that for a moment. But it's a relief... I've got them off my back.*

For many people, this sense of relief far outweighed the restrictions of being an undischarged bankrupt.

> *I'm aware of how bankruptcy does affect you but at the time, nothing was so great as the stress I was under and because I was young I thought I could overcome it. I just wanted to start again. I didn't care.*

It was very important that respondents felt that they gained something from bankruptcy. Where people did not experience this sense of relief, bankruptcy was a more damaging experience. One man, whose business affairs were relatively complicated and who had not been advised about bankruptcy, had the most negative views. He had to wait some time after he had declared himself bankrupt, while Official Receivers dealt with his case, to discover its full impact. Rather than put an end to his insecurity, bankruptcy had only contributed to his state of flux. He found this both infuriating and depressing. He explained:

> *The girl who was counselling me after [I'd gone bankrupt] said, 'Oh, you must feel a lot better now it's all off your shoulders.' I said, 'I feel no different at all because I don't know what it is. It's an animal. I've got an eight page booklet that told me nothing, from the official receivers. And the official receiver, I phoned one he told me one thing, a lady tells me another thing. You know, "You might lose this, or you might not. It just depends." So they might just as well give a little booklet that says "IT JUST DEPENDS".'*

PEOPLE WHO CHOSE NOT TO GO BANKRUPT

Those who did not go bankrupt had usually been advised not to do so by trained debt counsellors. This advice is normally given to people who either have too much, in assets, to lose by going bankrupt or whose debts are manageable without bankruptcy. People in this situation must work out an official Individual Voluntary Arrangement or an informal agreement with their creditors to pay off their debts.

However, there were a few people who had decided against bankruptcy, despite being advised that this was their best course of action. For many this was borne out of the strength of their commitment to 'pay for their own mistakes'. One said, *'No, it [bankruptcy] was suggested but I felt that I need to pay my debts...'* Another explained:

> *People outside [the situation]... were saying, 'You can, the situation you're in, you can declare yourself bankrupt and that would be one way to be rid of it. I said 'Well, no, I don't want to do that, I'd rather pay off my debts'. If the shoe was on the other foot, and someone owes me money, I wouldn't like them to declare themselves bankrupt and end up not paying me, so I'd rather pay the debts, even though it's difficult to pay. I'd rather do it that way.*

Others felt that, in their particular circumstances, bankruptcy could only create as many problems as it solved. One believed that the stigma of bankruptcy among his Asian community would have long-lasting repercussions for himself and his family.

> *I didn't want my suppliers to know... now for a family business like ours and with the community that we live in, those kind of rumours... could have been pretty detrimental to us you know. I'm from the Moslem Pakistani community, you know, and we've got a lot of respect amongst them, so I didn't want people to know that we were suffering financial difficulty...*

In fact, he was very angry even at the suggestion that he should think about bankruptcy.

> *Although that was the right advice to give me at the time, I didn't feel it was the right advice for me because...*

In addition, people who had been self-employed in a profession which they were hoping to pursue after self-employment were also particularly concerned to avoid bankruptcy. They all sold what they could of their businesses to recoup their losses and made informal agreements with their creditors to pay off the balance. They felt very strongly that bankruptcy would severely damage their professional reputation both in terms of their managerial ability and their financial integrity. Whether they continued to pursue their profession as employees or in self-employment, it was important that their reputation remained unblemished.

THE LONG-TERM FINANCIAL CONSEQUENCES OF SMALL BUSINESS FAILURE

In many respects, the long-term impacts of small business failure were broadly similar for all respondents regardless of whether they were trading or not trading, bankrupt or not.

For most, the key financial impact of small business failure was the uncertainty that it created in their lives. They often faced a great deal of change and upheaval at a stage in their lives which they had expected to be relatively stable. They also had to find other means of employment, often in new areas which did not utilise their skills or experience or which offered little security. Many had lost the homes that they had worked hard for and raised their families in. They faced the insecurity of private renting, at least for a while, until they got back on their feet. Further, many were unsure whether they would ever be granted a mortgage again.

In addition, many had lost the long-term financial security which they had been working towards. Most had lost all of their savings, which had been invested in the business or used to pay off their debts. Others had taken a range of steps to try to buy their business out of trouble, all of which damaged their long-term financial security. One couple had cashed in a pension worth around £14,000 when their business had started to experience serious problems. Another couple, in a desperate attempt to reduce their outgoings, had extended the terms of their £15,000 finance company loan from five to ten years. This reduced their repayments by almost £100 but the additional interest they would be paying meant that, in the long-term, they would have to make repayments totalling over £27,000. More importantly, they had cancelled the insurance policies on their loans and, without them, the long-term impacts of sickness or accident on their ability to repay the loans would be very serious.

Another respondent had sold a more successful business to try to prop up her ailing second enterprise. This business would have supported her and her family had they cut their losses and closed the failing company earlier.

Clearly, the older respondents were at the time their businesses failed, the greater this impact was. Older respondents, who had often been accruing financial security for their retirement, had a lot to lose in terms of their security. They also had less time before retirement in which to recover their losses. One couple said wearily:

> *I just don't know. I think we're the wrong side of fifty, if we were in our twenties we could easily get over this, but at our age we should not be thinking of finances that we owe. We both work now, full-time, and there's not a lot left at the end of it and I feel bitter about that.*

Another also felt the time he had hoped to enjoy in retirement, relaxing and spending time with his wife, was slipping away.

> *I mean I started when I was fifty-one, and I expected to retire at sixty-five like any normal personal would, with a bit of money in the bank... but it hasn't happened that way. I'm still struggling to survive now at sixty-six... to try and get myself in a position where I'm not getting kicked out of my house.*

Another couple had had to sell their cottage in France, where they had hoped to retire. The loss of this property, coupled with the fact that their financial situation made the possibility of any sort of retirement very remote for some years ahead, was a bitter blow.

Most respondents had had to change their lifestyle after their businesses failed, and some were living in quite severe hardship. It had been a long time since they were able to afford luxuries like new clothes or holidays. Buying gifts for birthdays and Christmas was a real problem for a few. One explained, '*We've struggled at Christmas...we've not swapped presents for several years now*'. Many also found that their social lives were severely constrained. One respondent had only two pounds a week left for discretionary spending. He said, '*I thought, "Well, how can I make £2 last the week?" I couldn't even buy a tin of beer*'.

Many were also having problems affording more basic expenses – they were cutting back on food and trying to reduce their utility bills. One had had to have their phone removed which caused her a great deal of anxiety:

> *We've been without the phone about five months now. We can't afford it. It was one item that I felt we could do without but we found now it's gone we miss it terribly... I worry about when they're at school, if there's a problem. I've had to give them next door's number. Also because Mum's not well, that's a worry as well.*

Others had sold their televisions because they couldn't afford the licence fee and feared the financial burden of a fine. People with children had often had to make the most serious adjustments to their lifestyles and felt that their children suffered disproportionately. One explained:

> *Things like buying shoes, buying clothes for them... and especially the oldest. She was at senior school in fourth and fifth year. All her friends were getting the latest trainers or latest shoes or latest dress or whatever, and she just had to make do with what she's got. And sometimes she wanted to go on a trip somewhere and we'd say, 'We can't afford it' and things like that.*

In the midst of these financial difficulties, some people also found themselves forced to rely on other people, which they found humiliating. One respondent had to accept food parcels from his parents-in-law so that at least his children could get a reasonable diet. Another had to depend on a relatively new partner for all his financial needs:

> *I mean, literally, we are very hand to mouth at the moment... I get to the point where I tear my hair out... I mean I like to buy the Gardeners World magazine once a month. I hate to say to Pauline, 'Have you got any money so I can buy the magazine?. I smoke a pipe, I don't smoke it a lot but I like a little smoke once in a while... and I can't stand asking people for that.*

A third respondent was faced with the knowledge that he would almost certainly have to ask his son for money but was very resistant to the idea:

> *If I'm desperate... I know I could go to my son... but I'd rather sweep the streets than do that.*

For some, the financial impact of small business failure was so severe that they found it a real struggle just to survive. A couple and their two children were desperately trying to make ends meet after their business had closed and they had been made bankrupt. They were not entitled to contributory benefits – unemployment benefit or sickness benefit – because they had not maintained their national insurance payments while they were self-employed. They were also unaware that they were entitled to means-tested benefits. Because her husband had suffered a nervous breakdown after the closure of the business and was unable to work, his wife had taken a low-paid night job. She said:

> *It was a nightmare, it really was...he wasn't entitled to any benefits at all because he'd missed some of his stamps, national insurance, because he couldn't afford it. And so when he finally was ill he wasn't entitled to any benefits at all. So we had nothing to live on except £89 per week that I brought in, which was a joke when I'd got a mortgage and everything else to pay.*

They had been allowed to remain in their family home for a period of grace before being required to sell the house under the restrictions placed on undischarged bankrupts. However, they had built up substantial mortgage arrears since the bankruptcy due to their lack of income. Consequently, they had been forced to try everything they could to raise money – including selling some of their possessions at a car boot sale.

> *We were that broke, one Saturday we got as much as we could ready to do a car boot sale because we hadn't got two pence in our hand left. I was trying to pay the mortgage, that was my main priority and after that to feed our family. And it rained and the car boot sale was cancelled and we all just sat here and cried because we hadn't got a penny... I know what it's like to hit rock bottom.*

Although things had begun to improve, as her husband had recovered enough to take a job, she still felt she had a long struggle ahead:

> *It was horrendous, and it took us twelve months to get anywhere and we're still struggling, really struggling now. It's touch and go all the time and the pressure's constantly on.*

It was this continual pressure and the constant insecurity of trying to make an insufficient income cover their outgoings that the respondent found hardest to cope with. She said:

... It would take such a lot of years of living like this to finally get somewhere... it depends how much I'm prepared to cope with here before I've had enough. Because it does...you get to a point where you just feel like giving up, you know, you're working, you're just working to pay your way. There's nothing else to look forward to at all. You just keep going and keep going but then every now and again you just think, 'It's not enough'. You want something more out of life than just working to pay the bills....

Summing up her situation, she remarked:

It's not a future is it, really? I don't see a future in it.

Chapter 5

The Personal Impact of Small Business Failure

As well as its devastating financial consequences, small business failure also has a serious impact on people's personal lives. Business problems and the decline into business failure can have grave implications for the physical and psychological well-being of the people involved. It can also undermine their self-esteem and the relationships they have with other people. Moreover, these impacts do not simply affect the people who are responsible for the business, but their families as well. In general, the personal consequences of small business failure were universal and affected the vast majority of respondents regardless of their different circumstances. There were, however, some distinctions in the extent to which small business failure impacted on their personal lives

IMPACT ON PHYSICAL AND MENTAL HEALTH

Self-employment can be a very pressured way of working, even without encountering business problems. In addition, the isolation of self-employment and respondents' emotional absorption with their businesses gave them few outlets for their anxieties. These factors clearly impacted on their physical and psychological well-being and very few people in our study had avoided suffering from a stress-related illness of some kind.

Many of the health problems that people suffered from were relatively minor, stress-related conditions, usually triggered by anxiety about business problems. However, some people, usually those whose businesses had actually failed, suffered more serious health consequences. A few developed quite serious conditions immediately after their businesses had closed, in a reaction to the stress involved in the run-up to business failure.

The run-up to small business failure

The vast majority of respondents reported some physical or stress-related symptoms which had developed during the period before their business closed, when they were struggling to cope with the problems they faced. Those who were still trading at the time of this research gave us a first-hand understanding of the health impacts of coping with business difficulties. In addition, many of the people who had closed their businesses by the time they were interviewed also located their health problems in the run-up to business failure.

Physical and psychological health problems were often non-specific and, therefore, difficult to alleviate. Many people attributed the onset of various symptoms – skin conditions, digestive problems, headaches and migraine, insomnia, ulcers and high blood pressure – to their high levels of anxiety during the run-up to business failure. One man in his early twenties whose music shop had closed down reflected:

> *... I think looking back on it, that I was ill probably for the six months before it all ended because I had so much that I had to handle...*

Another, whose pub had suffered severe financial difficulties before they were forced to close it, explained:

> *... it really made us ill, you know. It was on our minds all the time. You couldn't sleep properly for thinking about it or anything...*

Several people were prescribed medication to alleviate their symptoms, including anti-depressants and sleeping pills:

> *My blood pressure was way up, I had to go on beta blockers and so forth... I was on about five or six [types of medication]. I couldn't sleep without sleeping pills. And I would only sleep for two or three hours at a time and wake up with these awful fears and worries again at two or three o'clock in the morning, have to take some more pills to try and get another two or three hours sleep and be awake again at six o'clock, take another couple of pills. And then you've got the staff knocking on the door to come in and clean the place at eight o'clock in the morning.*

Levels of anxiety and, consequently, health problems, were exacerbated by two key elements of self-employment – physical strain and social isolation.

A key cause of health problems for many people was clearly the physical demands of running a business, usually single-handed. Self-employment was toughest for those whose businesses required hard and/or prolonged physical exertion. Those who ran shops, pubs and hotels were particularly likely to find that their physical health had been affected. They worked very long hours, usually without help, and were often unable to take a break during the day, even for meals. A pub landlord described his struggle to keep his business going:

> *Well, all I can say, at this stage... I'm working a sixteen hour day, seven days a week, eating one meal a day.*

Another man, who ran a carpentry business, explained the relentless effort it took to try to keep his head above water:

> *I usually work a good eight hour day, physically, and then come home and do the office work. Or you've got to go out and see somebody about another job. And you've got to get all the invoices typed up, end of the month, then you've got to sort out the VAT, write off all your cheques and things. All those things've got to be done at night or weekends.*

Long working hours, particularly over a period of several years, left people with little time to worry about their physical health or fitness.

The people who were most likely to find themselves in this position tended to be reluctant recruits and constrained choice entrants. However, some positive choice entrants and entrepreneurs also had physically demanding jobs. Poor physical health was, in fact, common for anyone whose business success was largely dependent on factors beyond their immediate control.

Those who ran businesses offering specialist services were in a relatively stronger position to weather a drop in trade and could adjust or expand the service they offered, try to market it more widely or, if necessary, offer it more cheaply. In contrast, others, such as people running shops, pubs or hotels had far fewer options to improve their circumstances. They were wholly dependent on people choosing to come to their business and then choosing to spend money. Most of their costs – premises, stock, equipment – were fixed and could not easily be reduced, particularly in the short-term. If strategies such as advertising and price reductions were unsuccessful, there was little action they could take other than try to reduce their outgoings. They achieved this by making any staff they employed redundant, working longer hours themselves and cutting down personal expenditure on, for example, food and leisure. These strategies clearly had an adverse impact on their physical health.

The demands of self-employment also meant that several people were forced to ignore existing health problems and, sometimes, to disregard medical advice. This had serious implications. One man explained how he had ignored his doctor's recommendation so that he could get back to work and keep his business going:

> *I had a heart attack about four years ago now... and since then I've had four bypass surgeries... and I've still carried on with the business... I couldn't work after the operation for three months – at least, that was the specified period. In actual fact, as soon as I could drive the car I was back at the office working on all the office side. And it weren't long before I was back working [outside] again...*

Another developed serious ulcers during the time he was self-employed but was unable to take enough time off work to give them a chance to heal:

> *I was seriously ill. I didn't know how ill I was at the time... I'd been going to hospital for about a month and they were treating me for haemorrhoids. But they found out in the meantime that there were ulcers, and they'd eaten part of the lower intestines away... I was going in and having operations... maybe once every month. And they told me that the only way they would get better is totally to pack in work. And, of course, I wouldn't...*

Although this enforced neglect of health problems meant that people could keep their businesses going in the short-term, it took a serious toll in the longer-term.

Often this reluctance to take time off work was exacerbated by confusion over entitlement to, or resistance to claiming, social security benefit. Research has identified a widespread, and erroneous, belief among self-employed people that they are not entitled to any social security benefits (NAO, 1993; Brown 1994). In addition, research has also found a striking resistance to claiming welfare benefits among self-employed people compared with employees (Blanchflower and Oswald, 1990). However, at the time this research was conducted, very little information was available to self-employed people about their entitlements to benefit (NAO, 1993).

Perhaps more problematic for self-employed people, is the fact that their claims tend to be extremely complex and can be very difficult for Benefits Agency staff to deal with. The quality and accuracy of advice offered to self-employed people about benefits was found to vary and the error rate in processing Income Support application forms for the [formerly] self-employed has been found to be high (NAO, 1993). Anecdotal evidence suggests that some self-employed people are told by Benefits Agency staff that they are not entitled to claim any benefits to cover periods when they are unable to work due to sickness.

Levels of stress and anxiety were also heightened by the isolation of self-employment, not simply because most people worked alone, but because they devoted all their time and energy to trying to save their business. More importantly, they usually went to considerable lengths to shield their families from the extent of their problems. As a result, many spoke of a deep need to simply talk their problems over with someone.

> *I [was] suffering from stress, depression, never to the extent that I actually needed to have any treatment for it but I did... see the doctor about it a couple of times. Just the fact that I'd actually sat and talked to him put it all into perspective really. I mean my wife and I talked about it... but when we were both low it was very difficult. I mean we'd always... tried to hide it from the children.*

This emotional strain and isolation seriously reduced respondents' ability to cope with the problems they faced.

One of the most frustrating aspects of small business failure for many people was the impact of stress and anxiety on their performance at work. Many were catapulted into a vicious circle whereby their ability to deal effectively with business problems declined as the extent and gravity of these problems increased. Several people who were still struggling to cope with business problems at the time of the research illustrated this very clearly. A salesman, whose business success depended heavily on his personality and charisma, told how the stress and anxiety of business problems was affecting his work:

> *I jump when the phone rings because I don't see it as somebody on there with some good news, I see it... as somebody with bad news and I don't want to answer it.... I go and call on people and I give them their quotations and what have you, and I say to them, quite happily 'I'll give you a ring in about a week' and I'll sit there with a list of people and I don't want to ring them... It's got nothing to do with the fact that I don't want to talk to them, it's the fact that I don't want them to reject me. I don't want them to say to me 'Sorry, I've gone somewhere else'... so I talk myself out of ringing them.*

Others told a similar story:

> *I can come into the office and find when I've left in the night that I've done very little. In other words, you can stare at things and not produce.*

After small business failure

We have seen that most people's health began to suffer in the run-up to small business failure. However, the health problems which developed after they had actually closed their businesses down tended to be considerably more serious.

Many spoke of feeling drained, worn out and even 'shell-shocked' during the period immediately after their businesses closed:

> *I haven't got the mental energy or the stamina any longer. I'm just trying to pull my life back together again...*

> *... I had no energy. The doctor told me I had to go for walks and that, and that would whack me. I'd get up in the morning, I'd have two or three hours up and I'd go to sleep and then I'd get up again and I'd go to sleep again...*

As well as feeling generally 'washed out', some respondents fell prey to quite severe viral infections immediately after they ceased to trade. Several contracted pneumonia, others got very bad doses of flu. One explained:

> *I was ill with some kind of virulent influenza... my doctor actually kept me off from the 1st January – it was an extremely virulent form of flu – until about the first week of March.*

In addition, a few people were so traumatised by the experience of small business failure that they suffered serious psychological problems after their businesses closed. Four people had suffered nervous breakdowns, illustrated by the case study below.

Some people had not fully recovered from nervous breakdowns, even some years after their businesses had failed. One respondent's wife had to explain her husband's circumstances because, more than two years after their butchers shop had closed, he was still too depressed and withdrawn to take part in an interview. She described his reaction to business failure:

> *... he'd just given up completely... he couldn't go out at all. If he went to the shops he was suffering panic attacks, especially in shops where there was tills and serving... he couldn't cope with the children, couldn't talk to me about it, just completely and utterly depressed, so the doctor that came said that he was very serious...she wanted him to go into hospital for a rest, and he wouldn't go in.*

Even by the time of the interview, his psychological state had improved only marginally.

Moreover, several people admitted that they had contemplated suicide.

In fact, one man who had been selected to take part in the study committed suicide shortly before the fieldwork began.

CASE STUDY 1

A young man explained how he had felt after watching the business he had dreamt of running decline slowly into failure:

...the moment it all stopped and it was all over... I just went... My doctor said that what I'd been doing was just cruising on auto all the way through it, trying to get through it on this, like, auto speed and as soon as I finally got the mess out of the way... my body just went..

He had suffered a complete nervous breakdown and the impact on his psychological health had affected every aspect of his life. He explained:

I would get up and because my wife was at work I'd have to tidy up. I'd have to, like, hoover, wash up and I'd have to keep a complete diary because I couldn't keep that many thoughts in my head. Because it would like, not confuse me, but it's a weird feeling, so I'd have to go back and do the hoovering and tick it off, and then do the dusting, so I didn't have to think of loads of things at once. I would forget things and then get upset.

If I was driving in the car and the lights were on red, I knew I had to stop and hold on the clutch or whatever, I'd start crying because of that, you know.

I couldn't go out, couldn't see friends, I couldn't go to a restaurant because I'd be sitting in the restaurant and I could feel this build-up that I'd have to get out into the air and space...

I just...well, I just wanted to end it all. I used to go and sit on a bench on one of those lanes in the early hours of the morning and I just used to look around thinking 'Well, what have I got myself into? What a hell of a mess I've got myself into'.

IMPACT ON SELF-ESTEEM

For the majority of people in this study, small business failure was one of the worst things that had happened in their lives. In particular, they found their lack of control over the events leading up to business failure very hard to bear. This made the experience very traumatic and, for some, more difficult to cope with. Many people found it even more difficult to deal with small business failure after the event than during it. One explained:

I mean, it didn't really hit me until afterwards because I'm the sort of person, if I'm in the midst of a crisis I just get in and get on with it. But it's afterwards... it's the aftermath more with me, I think. It affected me more afterwards than at the time, at the time your instinct is for survival...

Small business failure severely damaged people's self-image. The majority spoke of having no confidence, no self-worth, feeling defeated and humiliated. Many found it very difficult to talk to people about the business failure and lost interest in going out and socialising. Often they had a strong sense of their own failure:

I was convinced when I started that we would be okay... but by the time this was happening, everything went wrong, I felt so small, I felt terrible. I felt like, well, like a complete failure, I felt I was useless and it was all my fault...

Feelings of failure were particularly strong among women and when other family members were directly affected. One woman who felt she'd disrupted the lives of her whole family carried a strong burden of guilt:

Just a sense, I think, a feeling of, a big sense of being a failure, not just to me but to the whole family.

People whose businesses had failed often projected their poor self-perception onto their relationships with other people. Many believed that the experience had not simply affected them, but had also altered the way in which they related to other people, and vice versa. For them, small business failure was a very public humiliation. Case Study 2, opposite, provides a very clear picture of how small business failure can affect self-esteem.

In addition to their difficulties in relating to other people, many people were very angry with themselves for allowing their business to fail. They found it very difficult to come to terms with their own actions and behaviour during the run-up to business failure and some were unable to forgive themselves for the decisions they had made. It was not uncommon for people to express disbelief at their own actions during that stressful time. Others were consumed with guilt over what they perceived to be their own stupidity.

One remarked:

... it's a very strange business. I can't give you a totally analytical view of all this... because who can say why you do crazy things, you just do.

CASE STUDY 2

A 37-year-old, positive choice respondent was interviewed three years after the pub he and his partner owned had closed down. At the time he was interviewed, his strong sense of his own failure was still seriously affecting his social interactions.

> *Well, I don't hardly go out now, I feel like I've failed and if I see my friends and that, I know that they're talking about me failing, so I keep out of the way... I don't want to be talked about behind my back, you know, because if you try and explain it to them, the full situation, they don't understand. They stand talking to you and saying 'yes, yes' but they don't grasp the situation.*

His experience of small business failure had been particularly traumatic – he had been jailed for hitting a bailiff and had both his home and business possessed. He had found the whole experience very degrading:

> *Well, I've been to jail, I've never been to jail in my life, that's degrading enough, and then to be told you're going to be repossessed... and bailiffs coming round, it's degrading, you know.*

In addition, he had lost several of his friends and he believed that this was due to the business failure:

> *Well, it's funny about friends because when you're up they're all your friends, and when you're down you don't see many friends, don't get many people coming to see you or phone calls. When you're a landlord of a pub, you've got a lot of friends, or you think so...*

Further, his lack of self-confidence meant that he was still unable to put the experience behind him and move on:

> *My mother lives a hundred yards away from the pub and when I go past, I go past the other way... I don't want people seeing me, it's an embarrassment.*

Another was incredulous at his own decision-making:

> *... despite the fact that you're talking to an intelligible, intelligent, rational person now, I obviously couldn't have been then.*

One was so disillusioned with the way he, and those around him, had reacted to the business failure that he felt his self-identify had been undermined:

> ...*if you'd have told me five years ago that I would have lied the way I've lied... I would have said I was incapable of doing anything because I was such a nice guy. It's not me, and I've hurt so many people in different ways...*

An important element of the impact on self-esteem was the isolation that many people felt, stemming largely from their difficulties in confiding in other people. Many had spent a great deal of their time and energy trying to hide their situation from friends and, sometimes, their families. This added to the strain.

> ... *the shop, the shop, the shop, the shop, was all we ever talked about but we knew by now that things had gone wrong. But to other people [we said] 'Oh fine, fine, yeah, everything's going great, like, you know'. And we spent that long hiding it from other people and I think it was when you began to realise that other people would have to know that it really did strike home what you'd done, what you'd lost, what you'd gone through.*

Another verified the effort it took to keep up the pretence for as long as possible:

> ... *you try to hide things as much as possible, I think, from your own self, from those round you until it gets to the point where you can't and then when it does all come out... I think it's like anything, it's like alcohol, it's like drugs, you've got to accept it in your own mind...*

In one sense, this strategy helped them cope with business failure by confining it firmly within a private sphere. In the long run, however, it simply increased their feelings of isolation and inability to cope:

> *That was the thing, it was the loneliness, it was nobody to turn to at all... people didn't realise, nobody understood. I mean even my own sister... she couldn't understand it...*

Another remarked:

> *It was all on my shoulders. I never let them feel it.*

In most cases, people believed that, in addition to protecting their own damaged self-esteem, their secretiveness about their business problems was important for other reasons. Many harboured a strong instinct to continue to try to protect their families from the worst effects of small business failure and avoided discussing business problems even with their closest family. However, in most cases, hiding things from people they were close to only made things worse in the long run. One remarked despairingly:

> *I've done my damnedest... I've lied through my back teeth to people I've cared about a lot; to basically try and make sure everybody's alright. And in the end it doesn't help...*

A clear gender difference emerges here. In general, men were so ashamed at their inability to perform the traditional 'breadwinner' role, they were even unable to admit the extent of their problems to their partners.

> *I never told my wife the situation we was in, it was only two years later that she actually found out what went on... I think because of pride really, I mean that I'm out there earning money, well working, but not earning enough to help the family, to cover the finances. She used to come to me and say 'How are things going?' and I'd say 'Oh, it's not too bad'*

Women, on the other hand, wanted their husbands to be involved in the business and to help them solve their problems, but were frustrated when this help and support was not forthcoming.

> *He just carried on... I think because it was my idea to start the nursery, everything was my idea and I was at the forefront and running every- thing... he had his job and he was sort of doing his duty but... but yet I still didn't have the help and the support that I really needed for the business.*

Another woman had a similar experience:

> *Well, he just shut his mind to it, he wouldn't accept what was going on. Or else he would but he wouldn't let me know...he's very quiet, inside himself...*

The key element in understanding the personal impact of small business failure lies in the personalities of the people involved. Many of the people in this study were used to being independent problem-solvers and valued these traits in themselves. Consequently, they found it extremely difficult to admit that they had been unable to cope with business problems.

> *Because I've always been used to handling things. I've been in the*
> *police force, we've been in the services. I've always been able to say*
> *'Right, yes, the situation's da, da, da'... [and] I couldn't do anything.*

A knock-on effect of this was that people around them often expected more of them than was reasonable, relying on them to make all of the decisions and solve all of the problems. This pressure was often too much for them:

> *... during a lot of this, I've felt I'm the one everybody wants to blame.*
> *Whether it's my ex-director, and her family, the other people involved,*
> *mum and dad, her [wife's] mum and dad, my children, the other lady*
> *[respondent's mistress], her husband, her mum and dad, and all those*
> *different people.*

All of them, even the reluctant recruits, found it very difficult to admit defeat and to ask for help. They often felt that the experience of small business failure had tangibly altered their personalities and their roles in life. They found it very difficult to be positive about the future and longed simply to be 'normal' again.

IMPACT ON RELATIONSHIPS WITH OTHER PEOPLE

Although the impact of small business failure falls largely on those actually responsible for running the business, it clearly also affects the people around them. People with business problems or whose businesses had failed found that their experiences impacted on their personal relationships in two contexts. First, their relationships with friends or family members who were involved in the business suffered often irreparable damage. More significant, however, was the 'chain reaction' of small business failure on respondents' partners and immediate family.

Relationships with friends and family involved in the business

The people in our study who set up businesses in partnership with other people had always chosen close friends or members of their family as their business partners. Few considered the implications of business problems or failure for their relationships with their business partners and it was rare for them to separate professional from personal relationships. As a consequence, even the most stable of relationships were often damaged beyond repair by the failure of the business.

One man who had set up a business with a very old friend spoke of the loss of his friendship with his ex-business partner:

It was just a deterioration in the relationships between us. We were very good friends, we'd known each other since [we were] three or four and, I don't know, he just... he didn't just walk out but... I knew that something was up, you know, and he... just in the end, sort of like, left it. And then once he'd left I found out things after, about the business... that he'd sort of hidden before...There were things, like, I found invoices stuffed down the back of filing cabinets. I found a letter from the accountant querying Len's wages.

He was unable and, to a large extent, unwilling to try to salvage anything of his personal relationship with his business partner. He had decided to simply *'write the whole thing off to experience'*.

Breakdowns in business relationships were usually more serious when other family members were involved. Three respondents had brothers who were involved in the business, two of whom had legal partnerships. The third involved his brother in his struggling business on the understanding that he would invest some money. Again, even family relationships could not stand the pressures of small business failure. One person commented:

They usually say don't run a business with family don't they? That doesn't work out, so that's what happened really... I think he came in January and he finished in the August... it didn't work out at all... he just left on not very good understandings really...

Another argued with his brother-in-law who had been unable to raise the amount he had promised in order to buy himself into the business. The respondent had been relying on this money to meet some of his pressing financial commitments and could not forgive his brother-in-law for *'going back on an agreement'*. His wife explained what had happened:

... it caused problems with my brother, didn't it, I mean they ended up more or less having a punch up, which if you know them, they're not that sort. They're not violent men at all. They don't believe in that sort of thing but they were at each other's throats one night over it...

This relationship had fallen prey to tension caused by financial pressures which were not the fault of either party. In a more serious case, the failure of the business could be directly attributed to the actions of the respondent's brother, who had been taking money from the business to feed a gambling addiction. This had caused a rift among the whole family.

> *Eventually, I found out he was borrowing money from all over the place, my young brother. I knew he liked a bet, he liked a bet on a Saturday or something like that but I didn't know he was gambling to that extent. Not what I found out since, and I can understand that's where a lot of the money went in the end.*

Although, at first, the respondent had found it very difficult to come to terms with his brother's behaviour, he had started to re-build a relationship with him:

> *I mean, really, at first I was angry, really angry with him. But as time's gone by I think the anger goes down. I feel sorry for him in a way now... my youngest son hates the sight of him... oh, if he see him on the street he'd kill him, my youngest son.*

However, they had not been able to regain the relationship they had before their business problems:

> *He started changing a little bit... because he's come here a couple of times, Anthony has, but you can still see now, he's that nervous even when he walks in here. If he comes in here, he's only come a couple of times in the last twelve months... he knows... he's done wrong, and he's made a mess of all our lives.*

Impact on marital relationships

Small business failure not only affected individuals involved in the business and their families. It also shattered people's relationships with their spouse/partner. Although many of the people in this study had gone to great lengths to protect their families from the worst ravages of small business failure, their success was limited. In fact, some had caused more damage to their marriages by keeping the extent of business problems a secret from their partners. Further, some of the partners and children of people whose businesses had failed suffered physical and psychological problems themselves. In some cases, respondents' partners took part in interviews, although their children rarely did, and could present their perspective on small business failure themselves. In other cases, respondents described the impact on their partners and children.

The run-up to small business failure was very difficult for respondents' families who, while still affected, were powerless to intervene. Their inability to help and lack of control over the business caused them acute stress and anxiety which affected their physical and psychological well-being. One respondent's wife developed migraines during the run-up to small business failure. Another described this period as a time when her '*head was bursting with worry*' which she could not express, for fear of placing an even greater burden on her husband. Some respondents even felt that the impact of business failure was, in some respects, actually worse for their partners than for themselves because they at least had the business to focus on:

> ... *it was the wife really that needed more support than me... at one time I was frightened, I thought that she was heading for a heart attack or something.*

> ... *it was breaking her heart, you know, and the big thing is that her mental state of mind... with a history of mental health problems on her side of the family... I've been very concerned. She was literally capable of committing suicide... she was bloody close to it a couple of years ago.*

Often, however, the damage that small business failure caused to personal relationships was more serious than their health concerns. Respondents' relationships with their partners were almost always adversely affected by small business failure – whether they had been involved in the business or not. However, where both members of a couple were involved in the business, relationships were particularly vulnerable as they both tried to cope with the strain in their own way. One woman described how difficult it had been to watch her husband give up on everything they had worked for:

> ... *you don't see somebody work for X amount of years from scratch to get this dream going, and eventually he gets it...I could see him giving up and...I was cross with him... I wanted him to keep on fighting but I could see it in him, he'd had enough. Just, I think mentally, just mentally he'd had enough. He loved...we both did, we both absolutely loved the place.*

Many found that the enormity of the problems they were facing rendered them unable to talk to each other, often after many years of marriage.

> ... *it's affected our marriage, we can be virtually strangers some days. We love each other very dearly, very, very dearly, but we find now that we can't communicate because all you've got to talk about is doom and gloom... you just both go very quiet and reserved... it's not easy, and we have our very, very quiet moments and you feel as though you're drifting apart. And hopefully we won't...*

In some cases, these relationships were strong enough to weather the pressures and couples were able to '*help each other through*'. In the majority of cases, however, tension and depression eroded these relationships and both parties suffered. One respondent's wife explained:

> *If it had just been me and him, to be honest, I think we would have just fell apart. I think he'd have gone that way and I'd have gone the other. They could have took the house, the shop, everything, I wouldn't have cared. I don't think he would to be honest. But because we'd got these [kids] always asking, always demanding, always wanting something you had to deal with them before we could deal with each other. And by the time we'd dealt with them we both would just collapse, wouldn't we?*

Another couple, who did not have young children to hold them together, found that small business failure had an enormous impact on their relationship. They began to argue, particularly about money and the debts that were building up. The wife explained:

> *... he's a man that would not face a debt, he would put it to the side and hope by some miracle it'd go away. Whereas [I] would know that debt's not going to go away, and it's got to be brought forward. So it caused a terrible, terrible trauma in our marriage. Terrible arguments.*

Coping with small business failure also left couples with very little energy to invest in their relationship.

> *And the strain was really getting to me and I kept saying to him I need somebody to take the load off me, I need...and he wasn't in any fit state to do it...*

Respondents' feelings of guilt, described above, were of key importance in shaping the impact on marital relationships, particularly where shared assets, such as the home and personal savings, had been lost. It was not uncommon for respondents to feel that they had betrayed their partners by destroying everything they had worked and saved for.

> *... all that money's lost and she's virtually lost her home, so I can't blame her for...for the way she feels. She feels she's been betrayed and in many respects she has...*

This often made them unable or unwilling to discuss their concerns with their partners – either because they wanted to protect them, or because they felt their partner blamed them for the situation.

> *... he used to turn around and say 'Well, it's your fault' you know 'It's you'. I mean we'd always been close, but it ripped us apart.*

In fact, the most serious damage to personal relationships occurred when respondents tried to keep the extent of business problems to themselves – lying to their partners either directly or by omission. Not only did this mean that respondents' partners felt betrayed because they had been lied to, it also meant that they often did not find out the true extent of problems until the very last moment. One respondent's wife did not find out that the family business was in trouble until just a few days before their house was possessed.

> *... and it was a very difficult situation because when my wife found out about it, she found out about it a few days before we had to go to court to get the house repossessed. She just hit the roof really, she couldn't really believe it. It's...I suppose if she wasn't the sort of person she was perhaps we would have been divorced or something like that. But we sat down and worked things out, and we're here.*

This frequently caused more tension, as partners often felt that the situation may have been averted, had it been faced early enough:

> What annoyed me about Carol's situation, and the way she ran the business was that she never, ever, told me that she was in major problems... because if she had, they may have been able to have been sorted out earlier...

Often people only broke down and confessed how bad things had got to their partners when they could no longer cope with it themselves. This left their partners, usually wives, to try to pick up the pieces of a situation which they had not been involved in and often did not completely understand:

> *I was so angry because I wasn't kept in the picture of what was really going on... I think he was frightened of what he'd accumulated to be honest... everybody was fighting for their money and people were coming round to the house, as well, and I didn't know these people, never knew anything about it. And I'd have to sit down and listen to what was going on... I had to say 'Well, I'm sorry, but we haven't got it to give you'...*

This situation was, obviously, most common where only one marital partner was involved in the business. However, even couples who worked together in a business were driven to hide things from each other. This secrecy, undermining all the work that couples had invested in the business, resulted in even more recriminations:

> *We are different with money, so he probably wouldn't tell me about*
> *some of the debts from the shop because I would go absolutely berserk*
> *about it... where if I wasn't paying the bill, I would say 'I haven't got*
> *the money to pay this bill and I'm really worried about it' Ron would-*
> *n't particularly worry, so it would build up... There was a point when I*
> *thought 'I'll leave him' when I found out about the true debt on the*
> *shop. I thought 'I can't stand this, it's like a nightmare to me'.*

This lack of honesty, albeit motivated by a desire to shield partners and families from the worst of the problems, sometimes caused irreparable damage to relationships.

Impact on children

Business failure also had a serious effect on the health and well-being of respondents' children. Predictably, the impact of small business failure on children was greater where their mothers were involved in the business. Young children often developed problems associated with anxiety and insecurity such as bed-wetting, temper-tantrums and hysteria. Respondents identified these symptoms as a reaction to tension in the household and an attempt to get their attention. One said of her six-year-old son:

> *He's had nothing but ailments...emotional problems. I've had to go*
> *and see a psychologist with him and I think it was because, you know,*
> *Frank [her husband] had... gone so withdrawn that, of course, at that*
> *age they don't understand. I think he picked the tension up and his*
> *behaviour was... I think he realised...*

Another felt that her children had suffered because, in coping with her business problems, she had little time or energy left for them:

> *... because I wasn't there all the time and when I was at home I was*
> *always shouting at the kids or not paying enough attention to them. I*
> *was so tired all the time... My little boy was wetting himself because I*
> *wasn't around.*

Older children, in their early teens, who were still emotionally dependent on their parents, reacted more severely to the damage which small business failure wrought on their lives. They tended to focus their anxiety inwards and to behave in ways which were self-destructive. One young girl, who was old enough to be a confidante for her mother, but too young to be able to help, developed anorexia as she witnessed her mother's anxiety:

Natasha, she stopped eating, she was growing thinner and thinner and thinner...and she didn't get the A levels she wanted...

Two people emerged from the emotional trauma of small business failure to find that their teenage children had begun experimenting with drugs:

> *... my eldest son [had started] mixing with the wrong crowd and he was, until recently, a semi drug addict...He left school when he was sixteen and we wondered why he'd made a hash of his GCSE examinations, and we found out it was...it's one of these playground type of situations that started, and he went on to hard stuff and so on. So we had a lot of problems, smashed windows at home, my wife's engagement ring disappeared and cameras had gone.*

We cannot be certain that this was directly related to the impact of small business failure although the respondents themselves believed this to be the case. At the very least, however, they blamed themselves for being too preoccupied with coping with business failure to notice the changes in their children's behaviour, which were indicative of drug use.

> *It's not that we're naive [or thought] 'My daughter wouldn't do that' or we just said 'We don't care'... it's not that they're daft, or unintelligent, it's just...I don't know, it could have happened to us anyway... I think it's because, if you like, the family was at crisis point, all these problems were so exacerbated...*

Another respondent, whose son had developed schizophrenia during his late teens, recounted how the disruptions in his family, caused by small business failure, were exacerbating his son's condition.

> *... our younger son is a schizophrenic and he's quite ill... he's very ill, he's having a breakdown at the moment. All of these pressures have had a huge, well, it's affected the whole family but it's affected the schizophrenic more than most... Any threat to his home or any upsets with the husband and wife, the father and mother, affects him.*

People's relationships with their children were also deeply affected by small business failure. Those with young, dependent children simply felt that they had neglected their families and put the interests of the business before their children:

> *I used to work nine 'til five, he used to be at nursery all day and I used to get in... I was so tired, by the time I did my housework there was just enough time to put them to bed. So there was no quality time to spend with the children, and they were used to having me there, spending time.*

Certainly, the disruption to marital relationships caused by small business failure was very difficult for younger children to cope with.

> *And Bethany... she was about eleven or twelve at the time, she was suddenly seeing family that had always been together just being ripped apart by circumstances that I couldn't control.*

Not surprisingly, these guilt-feelings were felt particularly by women, although men, too, often felt that they had 'let their children down'.

People with older children felt that their relationships had been affected in different ways. Some felt that their inability to cope with their business problems had made them rely too heavily on their children for support:

> *Natasha was doing her A levels at the time and she used to come home, I would be trying to say to her 'Well, I can't do it, I can't see how I can make ends meet'.*

Others felt that they had lost their children's respect. This was particularly prevalent among men, who felt that, ultimately, they had failed their families and let down the people who relied on them the most. This made it very difficult for them to relate to their children. One man commented with great sadness:

> *Yes, it has obviously...they've seen their father fail, it's obviously hurt them. Certainly my son, very much... it's obvious, I can see that his respect for me isn't what it used to be.*

They felt they had lost their feeling of 'natural' seniority over their children and, therefore, sacrificed the right to expect their respect and admiration.

Impact on the family unit

Few of the people in this study had not experienced a negative impact either on themselves or those around them. Yet the sheer enormity of the impact of small business failure cannot really be appreciated simply by assessing its separate effects on the range of people involved.

Often the stress and trauma involved completely undermined respondents' perceptions of their own role in the family and, more importantly, their ability to relate to other family members. This resulted in the worst effects of small business failure. Unable to allow their families to watch them suffering, and unable to cope with the anguish

CASE STUDY 3

A young, male respondent had suffered a severe nervous breakdown after his business had failed. He simply felt unable to deal with his own problems as well as providing his partner with the emotional commitment and support he felt she deserved. As he was unable to help her through it, he felt duty-bound to protect her from it, by removing himself from the household.

'I think because at the time, I think the breakdown... I hadn't just suddenly got at that stage, I'd been ill miles before that, you know... Caitlin was very supportive, Caitlin was very good and she knew there was something up. She knew it was wrong, the pressure was there, but, I don't know, at the time... [I was] keeping her out of it, and protecting her as much as I can from it. And my idea was actually,[that] the best way I can keep her from suffering, or any loss was actually to push her away, and get her out of it... If I broke the relationship then she'd be okay because she'd be on this side of the fence, away from everything that was happening to me. And that's what happened. Now I realise I should have used Caitlin for the support she was and I suppose it wouldn't have been as bad as it was. In the end, I went back to my parents, but originally I moved somewhere, which was a bad decision, to go off on my own. With nothing, with no one, I did all the wrong moves... nobody knew where I was... at the time I never realised but when I look back, well, I was just in a state.

CASE STUDY 4

F: *Things broke down between Tim and me and, really. Where was I when he needed me? I was going through my own trauma... I'd got my own trauma... The financial side was affecting us both, I had nothing to do with it, on paperwork I was just an employee... And so, yes, you know, things were fraught... it just broke down in one complete vicious circle. And then, like I say, at the end of it, it's like, where was I when he needed me?... Someone was there.*

M: *I'd started an affair with somebody... Well, Sophie became aware of the affair and we tried to potter on, did our own thing. It was quite traumatic for us both, and is still, isn't it?*

F: *He desperately needed counselling because emotionally, financially... he was losing himself... he was losing himself completely. He was beginning to wonder who he was and what he was worth.*

M: *I tried to protect you somehow... I'm still coming through it. I feel my shell's still there and I tried to explain to Sophie that, in order to get my shell there, I've also had to distance myself somewhat from people I care a lot about. I've got no relationship basically with my daughters, my mother and father-in-law. I'm still trying to come through the other side of that area, but I need to have the strength to do it.*

CASE STUDY 5

One respondent's partner explained,

> *I wanted him to go in [to hospital]... but he said he'd prefer to stay at home. And I wanted him to go because I was finding everything too much... I just didn't know which way to turn. I was trying to go to work and keep them [the children] out of the way. I mean, we'd got no money, it was a nightmare, it really was...*

Things had not improved for this family, even more than a year after the business had closed. She was becoming increasingly resentful at being left to cope with the situation after their business had failed.

> *It's just very difficult... we just plod on, you know, for the sake of the children... it could have been so easy to just say 'Let's call it a day' and let it go.*

She was unsure how much longer she could tolerate the situation and had seriously considered leaving her husband.

> *Yes, most definitely. I told Greg, it's just...its been so horrendous. I think you feel if it's all got to go, then I just couldn't handle any more and I'd rather just sort myself out and start again. That's how I feel really, it's too, an awful lot. I mean maybe in time it might get better, but I find it very hard to tolerate. I mean I knew last year it was understandable but twelve months on my patience has worn off really... that's basically it, he's in his little world and I'm in mine.*

The pressure on her was made worse by the fact that the people around her, on whom she relied for support, had lost patience and interest in her situation.

> *I think people just lose interest, to be honest... everybody knows the situation but it's like it's exhausted itself for them so they don't...you're on your own, you're literally on your own.*

Further, some of her closest family had lacked understanding in the first place.

> *I mean, my family, they could have helped us, but they haven't... My dad, he's quite financially secure and... last year when all this was going on he just sort of said, 'Well, he'll have to pull himself together, he's got a wife and two children to support'. I think that side of it hurt more than anything because you need people to turn to, even to just sit and talk...*

This isolation made the situation even harder to cope with.

> *... people just don't understand what it's like, week in, week out. It's a different world to what they're living in, it really is.*

---

they felt they had caused, some people felt compelled to distance themselves – physically or psychologically – from their families. At its worst, small business failure resulted in a complete dislocation of household relationships and family life. This has to be viewed in its entirety for its impact to be fully recognised, as Case Study 3 on page 121 shows.

Another respondent (Case Study 4) told a very similar story of the need to distance himself from the people he cared about before he could begin to cope with the effects of small business failure. Further, his wife, who also took part in the interview, explained how difficult she had found it to support her husband during the business failure. Each of them clearly felt that they had failed each other.

In both of these cases, the couples involved had managed to resolve the worst of their problems and were living together again. The events around small business failure had seriously dented their relationships but they were hopeful of being able to salvage their relationships and, ultimately, their family life.

However, the future did not look as bright in Case Study 5 (page 122). This respondent had also distanced himself from his partner but, unable to do so physically, he had suffered a nervous breakdown resulting in almost total psychological withdrawal from family life. The consequences of this withdrawal were harder for his family to cope with and more long-term. His wife undertook most of the interview as her husband was still unable to engage in prolonged social interaction.

At the time of this interview, it was unclear whether the family would be able to survive small business failure or whether the impact would simply be too much for them to bear.

Conclusion

Discussion of Findings

This exploratory study into small business failure illustrates that it has a deep, and often very damaging, impact on everyone who is involved in it. This includes not only the person who is responsible for running the business, but also their business partners and associates, their friends, their spouses and even, perhaps especially, their children.

The most damaging consequences of small business failure are not monetary, although the financial impact can be devastating. In fact, it is the potential for small business failure to shatter self-esteem, undermine personal relationships, destroy marriages and dislocate family life which are the worst effects. For the owners of small business, failure is a huge personal, as well as professional, blow, representing the death of a dream. Often, however, the casualties are those who were not involved in the business at all, and it is this lack of influence in the chain of events surrounding business failure with renders their situation so difficult to bear. In extreme cases, children, who are often the most powerless victims of small business failure, are driven to self-harm because the only environment over which they have any control is their own.

If this study highlights anything, it is that the human dimension of small business failure is equally, if not more, damaging than the economic and financial impacts. If these effects are to be alleviated, a recognition of this human dimension must be reflected in debates of the advantages of self-employment; in all consideration of the implications of business failure; and in the help and support which is made available to self-employed people before they set up in business, while they are in operation, and after they close down. Several important lessons can be learned from this research which can inform this process.

ROUTES INTO SELF-EMPLOYMENT

It is usually assumed that people become self-employed by choice, and while this may be true, it is important to recognise that the choice may not always be free or informed. A high proportion of people in this study had very restricted opportunities when they started their businesses and many may never have considered self-employment if other options had been available. It is highly likely that these circumstances influence the likelihood of success.

Reluctant recruits, for example, had no other choices available and entered self-employment largely out of desperation, perceiving few advantages in doing so, other than that it offered some form of paid employment. Constrained choice entrants, on the other hand, had some alternatives when they were making their decision, but had tended to be vulnerable as employees, suffering multiple redundancies, workplace discrimination or bullying. Consequently, self-employment may not have crossed their minds had their options been more desirable. Yet, in starting their own business, they believed they had obtained the security and independence they required in their working lives.

Even the entrepreneurs, who conformed most closely to traditional stereotypes of self-employed people, were often not entirely free to choose the employment status which suited them best. Some did not have the temperament to bide their time as employees before they achieved their goal of autonomy and financial reward. Others, however, such as taxi drivers, building workers and market traders, were unable to work in any other status than self-employment. Only positive choice entrants displayed any real freedom of choice around self-employment, usually entering it from relatively secure employment and with marketable skills. Yet even people in this group had required a 'trigger' before they had begun to think about setting up a business.

Consequently, very few of the people in this study had the skills or experience they required to set up successful enterprises, and many were completely unprepared for the harsh realities of self-employment. The availability of more comprehensive information about the realities of self-employment could have avoided, or at least better prepared them for, some of the pitfalls they would face. Courses in business accounting and book-keeping are not always sufficient preparation for self-employment, and some people did not receive any training in these areas. A wider recognition of the skills required to run a successful business and of some of the problems likely to arise, could prevent people from making unwise decisions about self-employment and better prepare them for the rigours of being an 'entrepreneur'.

It also needs to be recognised that, particularly given the different routes into self-employment, people face very different risk factors, according to the context in which they were making decisions about setting up a business. This study clearly illustrates that routes into self-employment can transform the meaning and experience of self-employment for people in different circumstances.

Some of the respondents in this study were able to set up businesses which potentially offered higher economic returns than employment, allowed them to pursue a profession or trade in their chosen career and develop new and existing skills. For them, self-employment offered the personal satisfaction of building up a business in an area in which they knew they were skilled or in something which they were interested in. For most people, this is what self-employment is traditionally perceived to mean.

However, a significant proportion of the people in this study had a very different experience of self-employment. They entered it with reluctance or from a position of disadvantage and, subsequently, experienced more restrictions on their choices when they became self-employed. Due to their employment history and the absence of saleable skills or qualifications, they were forced to set up enterprises which certainly did not conform to the glamorous image of 'running a business'. They offered low financial returns while also demanding heavy physical labour and much longer hours of work.

These differences have serious implications for the level of satisfaction people attained from running their businesses and also for their chances of success. Even without business problems, the potential rewards – personal and financial – were far lower for the reluctant recruits and constrained choice respondents than for the positive choice and traditional self-employed.

These differential chances and risk factors also need to be recognised, both in the advice and information offered to people who are considering setting up a business and in the counselling offered to people who are self-employed.

FINANCIAL ARRANGEMENTS IN SELF-EMPLOYMENT

Organisations that work with self-employed people who have business problems agree that keeping business and personal finances separate is a prerequisite for good financial management. Yet this study clearly demonstrates that many self-employed people whose business failed were not fully aware of the need to maintain this distinction and, consequently, very few were successful in doing so. Some were completely unaware of the need to separate business and personal finances, or actively chose not to do so. The majority of the people in this study, however, either mistakenly believed that they were keeping business and personal finances separate or were unable to maintain a distinction despite setting up quite rigorous accounting procedures. As a result, small business failure results in a build-up of serious personal debts as well as business liabilities.

There are several reasons why the need for this separation is not fully recognised; why the distinction may, in any case, become blurred, in practice; and why attempts to keep business and personal finances apart are unsuccessful.

First, because few people were able to set up a small business without drawing on personal wealth or securing loans on their personal equity, personal finances were often intrinsically linked with business finances from the outset. In addition, people often borrowed heavily or unwisely in secured loans in order to set up their businesses and this had long-term consequences for the way in which they managed their finances while they were trading.

Second, as well as using personal money to set up their business, the majority of people also invested significant amounts of their own money into the business while it was running. Sometimes this took the form of further secured borrowing but, more often, it was informal and incremental. A key source of ongoing investment into small businesses among people in our study was from forgone wages that should have been drawn from the business. This, too, contributed to the build-up of personal liabilities.

Third, for some self-employed people, especially those who work from home or whose business profits are seasonal, there are few perceived advantages to keeping business and personal finances separate.

Fourth, maintaining a meaningful distinction between business and personal finances is clearly a more complex process than people generally understand it to be. It is not sufficient simply to have separate accounts, maintaining the distinction in practice is crucial if financial problems in the business are to be contained and prevented from undermining personal financial security. Yet, even among people who recognised the need for a practical distinction, the financial pressures which self-employment brought sometimes made it impossible for them to maintain it.

While it is not possible to identify a single, conclusive factor which explains why business and personal finances are inextricably linked in many small businesses it is possible to identify a number of indicators which influence the extent to which it is likely to occur. These include routes of entry into self-employment and levels of experience in running a business; nature and extent of financial commitments; the extent to which people anticipated high financial returns from self-employment; and the structure and nature of the business.

The most important factor, however, in encouraging people to keep their business and personal finances separate was having a third party, particularly a spouse, who was responsible for keeping the accounts. This process opened accounting procedures up to a scrutiny which many business accounts did not receive and required people to account for any personal money which was being ploughed into the business.

Unpicking the financial arrangements of self-employed people has furthered our understanding of how and why the confusion between business and personal finances occurs. This knowledge can inform advice to people who are setting up businesses as well as those with businesses that are already in operation. A clearer picture of the sources of confusion, and the points at which obstacles to maintaining a distinction are likely to occur, can ensure that advice and information can be more sensitive to both the timing and nature of people's needs in this area. If more people could be encouraged and helped to keep a distinction between their business and personal finances, the financial impacts of small business failure, at least, could be alleviated.

EXPERIENCES OF BUSINESS FAILURE

People's experiences of self-employment and the circumstances in which they made the decision to close down their business were crucial factors in determining the overall impact of small business failure. In most cases, small business failure was not a single event but the culmination of a long process. As the findings have illustrated, the factors which set the context for small business failure were:

- routes into self-employment;
- people's ability to cope with running a business;
- the nature of the business they were running; and
- financial circumstances.

People rarely made an economic decision to close their business, tending to continue long after it ceased to be financially viable because of their strong emotional attachment to it. Coming to terms with the idea of closing their business often took a long time and many people found the process very draining emotionally.

Only a very small group of people made a strategic decision to close the business before their losses became too great. The majority, however, struggled on, trying to retain their businesses for as long as possible. Some eventually experienced a 'trigger' event which forced them to close the business. Others simply continued until they were too physically or emotionally exhausted to carry on. A number of people were still struggling at the time of the research. Although most recognised that the chances of their business surviving were very slim, they were unable to stop fighting to save it. Many were, in fact, hoping for triggers which would take the decision out of their hands.

It is crucial that everyone involved in advising or counselling small businesses should be aware that, for many, the enterprise will be more than simply a means of earning a living. The personal investment which people made into their businesses, and their emotional attachment to them, was striking and these factors frequently clouded professional judgement. Consequently, it is equally, if not more, important that the emotional factors around running, and closing, a small business are addressed by small business advisors, as well as the economic circumstances. Many people are ill-equipped, both emotionally and professionally, to deal with business problems before they became insurmountable. Equally, some will prefer to wait until an external factor or a third party triggers the closure of their business, rather than do so themselves.

The emotional and physical trauma of this 'Russian roulette' approach to business problems and the financial consequences of people's unwillingness or inability to cut their losses earlier, are among the worst impacts of small business failure. Without recognising the paralysing effects of business problems for many self-employed people, business counselling and advice services are likely to have very limited success in alleviating these effects.

THE FINANCIAL CONSEQUENCES OF
SMALL BUSINESS FAILURE

Small business failure had a devastating, and often long-term, impact on the financial security of the people involved. Self-employed people facing insolvency usually have two options. They can decide to make themselves bankrupt or they can set up a Individual Voluntary Arrangement with their creditors which allows them to pay off their debts and avoid bankruptcy. Decision-making around bankruptcy was a crucial factor in shaping the financial impact of small business failure.

The people in this study had accumulated substantial losses and built up high levels of both business and personal debt as a result of small business failure. Many of these debts had accrued as people had struggled to keep their business afloat after the point at which it ceased to be viable financially. Most people had initially fallen behind with payments relating to their business and had then accrued personal debts by trying to prop the business up with their own money. Mortgage arrears were the most serious problems and many people had either lost their homes or were living in fear that they would be possessed by their creditors.

Just under half of the people we interviewed whose businesses had failed had made themselves bankrupt, the remainder set up Voluntary Arrangements or informal agreements with their creditors. Several people had tried to set up Voluntary Arrangements but had found that their creditors refused to accept them and they were forced into bankruptcy. In general, people refused to think about bankruptcy until their circumstances were really desperate, but most found it less traumatic than they had anticipated. For many, bankruptcy was a relief which allowed them to 'wipe the slate clean' but a few, particularly those who had been forced into bankruptcy by their creditors, were very bitter about it.

The most traumatic impact of bankruptcy, for most people, was the loss of their home. Many were renting properties in the private sector at the time of the research, only one family were eligible to be housed by their local authority. Other people were still waiting to find out whether or not they would lose their home and found this uncertainty very difficult to endure. Some people, mostly the entrepreneurs, expressed frustration at the financial restrictions placed on undischarged bankrupts, but many were relieved that they did not have the opportunity to build up any more debt.

For some people, however, it was the stigma and uncertainty of bankruptcy which had the most impact on their lives, rather than the practical restrictions on their activities. A few people had actually decided, against the advice of specialist debt counsellors, not to go bankrupt because they wanted to fulfil their responsibilities to their creditors or avoid the stigma and long-term financial consequences of bankruptcy. These people usually faced long years of financial hardship as they struggled to repay their creditors.

The research suggests, then, that the financial consequences of small business failure could be limited by an early recognition of the causes of some of the worst consequences.

Clearly, many of the financial consequences, especially those relating to personal financial security, stem from the failure to keep business and personal finances separate. This, again, points to the importance of educating self-employed people in the procedural and practical steps which have to be taken to ensure that this occurs. In addition, offering real examples of the way in which mixing business and personal finances can exacerbate the consequences of small business failure could provide a powerful incentive for people to try and maintain the distinction.

It is also clear that delays in making decisions about business closure and bankruptcy are a key contributor to the financial consequences of business failure. Much of this relates to a lack of knowledge about the procedures and outcomes of bankruptcy. Consequently, the prospect of bankruptcy loomed, for many people, like a horrifying spectre which signified their failure. In reality, however, most people found it a far less traumatic experience than they had anticipated. Equally, most people found the longer-term impacts of bankruptcy easier to live with than they had expected.

People who had received some advice and information about bankruptcy, in advance of experiencing it, were clearly in the best position to make decisions and to cope with the ordeal. Understanding the factors which had to be considered in their decision-making; knowing what to expect; and having some idea of the long-term implications was very empowering for some people. This not only gave them the confidence to make the decision, but also to feel that they had made the right choice. People who had not received advice until after they had decided about bankruptcy did not, on the whole, enjoy this peace of mind.

If comprehensive and easy-to-understand information about debt and personal insolvency were made available to everyone involved in running a business, preferably before they actually need it, it could make a big difference in containing the financial impact of small business failure. People experiencing business problems should also be encouraged to seek advice on personal insolvency and appropriate advice services should be available to them. Reducing the fear and uncertainty which most people felt about bankruptcy, prior to experiencing it, could make a significant contribution to ensuring that they were better able to make an informed choice and cope with the consequences.

THE PERSONAL CONSEQUENCES OF SMALL BUSINESS FAILURE

While the financial consequences of small business failure were serious and likely to have long-term implications, they were, perhaps, not as damaging as the personal impact on the people affected by it. Small business failure frequently had a profound effect on people's health, self-esteem and relationships with other people. It also impacted on the health and well-being of other family members.

Health

Many people developed stress-related conditions during the run-up to small business failure. Key factors which affected health and well-being included the physical demands of running a business and the social isolation of self-employment. Several people also developed more serious physical and psychological health problems after their businesses had closed and four suffered complete nervous breakdowns.

Physical health is, for self-employed people, as crucial to the success of their business as their product, the market and their sales figures. Yet the pressures of self-employment *per se* and, in particular, the problems associated with business failure, are extremely damaging to health and, consequently, reduce their ability to make the business work. Self-employed people must be encouraged to protect their health, if necessary by taking out health insurance which will cover them should they need to take time off work. Further, physical health problems are as endemic among people experiencing small business failure as debts, mortgage arrears and low self-esteem. They ought be recognised as a symptom and outcome of business failure and treated as such. It is as critical that people take time to rebuild their physical health after small business failure as it is to regain their financial security.

Self-esteem

Small business failure often undermined people's self-esteem, making it harder for them to relate to other people. In particular, they tried to shield their families from the extent of the problems. Consequently, many people felt very isolated.

Damage to self-esteem is an equally devastating outcome of small business failure. It undermines people's ability to deal effectively with business problems, make decisions about closure and bankruptcy and cope with the aftermath. It is unlikely that loss of confidence over something as serious as small business failure will be completely avoided and, again, this should be taken into account by advisors and other people involved with failing businesses. Similarly, marital and family problems should also be viewed as direct consequences of small business failure, rather than as the product of the stress involved in these circumstances. All of these factors are outcomes of small business failure and, if they are recognised and treated as such, may ensure that all of the effects can be recognised and alleviated before they become irreconcilable.

Personal and family relationships

Several people who had set up business with friends or family members found that these relationships broke down under the pressures of small business failure. Some felt it unlikely that these relationships could be repaired. In addition, marital relationships were almost always adversely affected by small business failure and some people were unsure whether their marriages could survive the strain they had been under.

People who had young children found that small business failure often impacted on them as well. Several reported that their younger children had developed behavioural problems as a reaction to the tension and anxiety in their home. Older, teenaged children were equally vulnerable and some had developed quite self-destructive behavioural patterns. Several people whose businesses were struggling or had failed felt that their relationships with their children had been affected, and men, in particular, were inclined to believe that they had lost their children's respect. In a few extreme cases, small business failure dislocated the whole family unit as people felt that the only way they could come to terms with it was to impose some distance – geographical or psychological – between themselves and their families.

Most of the people in this study had, with the benefit of advice and counselling, begun to repair some of this damage. Some, however, were still struggling to reach this point. Those who contemplated suicide may never have had the chance to re-build their self-esteem or their personal relationships. Certainly, the man who died while this research was being conducted never had the opportunity. This is an extremely high price to pay and, again, some lessons can be learned from this research which may avoid some of the worst costs of small business failure.

CONCLUDING REMARKS

Perhaps the strongest message which emerges from this research is that small business failure is an extremely complex issue, resulting in a huge variety and combination of outcomes. It is not, and cannot be treated as, a simple issue of debt or bankruptcy. The whole range of effects of small business failure needs to be recognised, addressed and alleviated, otherwise recovery from the experience may never be complete. The introduction to this report raised the fact that traditional advice services are usually inappropriate for the needs of people experiencing small business failure. It is pertinent to return to it here.

To date, only two organisations in the UK have recognised and sought to address the unique collection of problems faced by people running small businesses. Traditional advice and support services can only deal with particular problems caused by small business failure, usually in isolation from each other, rather than take a holistic approach. Business Debtline and Small Traders Advice Centre and Support (STACS) were set up specifically to fill this gap in advice provision.

Business Debtline was launched in the autumn of 1992 by the Birmingham Settlement, a voluntary organisation known for its pioneering approach to personal debt counselling. This service, dealing specifically with problems associated with small business failure, was set up in response to the growing numbers of clients who had suffered, or were experiencing, small business failure. Similarly, the STACS was also launched in 1992, growing out of an advisory service for self-employed people, set up by someone who had personal experience of small business failure.

Both of these organisations were created to tackle the whole range of financial and personal problems which arise from small business failure. They offered a telephone helpline as well as one-to-one counselling for people presenting serious or complex problems. Advisors were able to deal with people whose businesses were still running, as well as those whose business had failed, and operated a referral system for legal and accountancy services. They combined this with a recognition of the stress suffered by individuals and families as a result of small business failure. In fact, STACS very quickly identified a need for personal and family counselling as part of their advice service.

The Business Debtline and STACS were set up to cover specific geographical areas – Birmingham and Nottinghamshire, respectively – and they were unable to deal with anyone not living or working in these areas. An absence of available funding meant that they were unable to extend beyond these boundaries. Yet despite these restrictions, both organisations were inundated with requests for advice and counselling from very early in their existence. In fact, when the fieldwork for this research took place, neither organisation felt they could advertise their services more widely for fear of building up large back-logs of work.

There is clearly a need for advice services of this sort in other parts of the country. It is important to remember that, despite the depth and breadth of problems that some of the people who took part in this research had suffered, they are likely to be the 'lucky ones'. They were people who had received some sort of advice and counselling at some stage during their experiences of small business failure. A great many people, who were not living or trading in one of the areas covered by Business Debtline or STACS, are unlikely to have gained access to any appropriate advice services. We do not know how small business failure has affected them.

Yet STACS was forced to cease operating in September 1997 due to a lack of funding, leaving just one organisation in the whole of the UK to offer advice and support for people, living or working in Birmingham, whose businesses have failed. There are no advice services to deal with the problems of small business failure anywhere else in the country. The people in our research consistently spoke very highly of both STACS and Business Debtline. The vast majority of them firmly believed that without the help and support they had received, they would not have been able to cope. There was also a clear view, among the people we interviewed, that their circumstances could have been considerably worse had they not received advice.

It would seem that there is a strong case for ensuring that organisations like STACS and Business Debtline are given the political and financial support necessary to offer these crucial advice services to everyone who is suffering from small business failure, regardless of where they live or work. Further, if these organisations were in a financial position to offer a more proactive service, before business problems become insurmountable, some of the worst impacts of small business failure might not simply be alleviated, but avoided altogether.

Appendix

Research Methods

The research was based on forty depth interviews with people who had recently experienced business difficulties or whose businesses had failed. Twenty-seven of the interviews were with people whose businesses had closed down. The remaining interviews were with people who had contacted an advice agency due to business problems but were still trading at the time of the research. The fieldwork took place in Birmingham and Nottinghamshire.

THE SAMPLE

Respondents were identified through the records of Business Debtline and the Small Traders Advice Centre and Support (STACS), the only specialist advice services for small businesses in the country.

THE PILOT STAGE

Due to the exploratory nature of this study and the lack of existing information on the situations of people whose businesses fail the pilot stage was a crucial element of the research. Pilot interviews with eight respondents were carried out by the researchers. Originally the research was to include only people whose businesses had failed and the pilot sample reflected this. Staff at STACS selected and contacted ten clients whose businesses had failed, including a range of different types of business and reasons for business problems. Eight of these clients agreed to take part in the research and pilot interviews were carried out in late June 1995.

THE MAIN STAGE

The respondents for the main stage of the study were selected from clients taken on by Business Debtline or STACS for in-depth casework since June 1993. For reasons of confidentiality Business Debtline and

STACS were not able to provide a list of clients' names and addresses for PSI to contact. Instead we used an 'opt-in' procedure – that is, Business Debtline and STACS forwarded letters to their clients, on PSI's behalf, inviting those who wanted to take part in the research to complete and return a reply slip to PSI.

The letters introduced both PSI and the research project and stressed that Business Debtline and STACS were supporting the research. The letters were carefully worded in recognition of the emotional fragility of some of the people we were contacting. The letters also had to be sensitive to the loss of dignity and self-esteem suffered by people whose businesses are in difficulty or have failed. Consequently, the letters avoided using words such as 'failure' or bankruptcy. In addition, rather than describe the research as a study of 'business failure', the letters used more general terms and introduced the research as 'a study of self-employment and business difficulties'. The letters offered a £10 postal order as an incentive for taking part in the research.

The reply slip asked respondents to indicate:

- their age and sex;
- the nature of their business;
- their presenting problem at the time they contacted Business Debtline or STACS;
- the year they had started the business;
- whether or not they were still trading; and
- if not, when they ceased to trade.

Respondents were then asked to provide a name, address and contact number so that an interview could be arranged.

In recognition of potential low response due to a reluctance to talk about business problems or business failure we asked Business Debtline and STACS to contact all post-June 1993 clients rather than employ detailed sampling criteria. In total four hundred and three clients were contacted. Our initial caution proved to be justified – replies were received from fifty three clients. Seven of the fifty three clients who agreed to take part in the research could not be used in the main stage sample – three had moved some distance away from the fieldwork areas after their businesses had closed; four did not provide their name and address although they did complete the rest of the reply slip and return it to us. The remaining forty six names and addresses were issued to interviewers.

Interviewing took place in July, August and September 1995. Fieldwork progressed smoothly and interviewers attempted to contact everyone in the sample to give them the chance to participate (see Table A.1). Of the forty six people in the final sample:

- One person refused to take part although this was not due to lack of interest. This person had expressed interest in being interviewed but his business was still trading and pressure of work meant that they were unable to arrange a convenient time for the interview to take place.
- One person who had expressed a desire to take part in the research died during the fieldwork period, shortly after the sample had been drawn.
- Four were non-contacts which, given the high proportion of home repossessions after small business failure, was anticipated. A number of people in the sample moved during the fieldwork period but were able to keep in touch so that interviews could be arranged. Interviewers never managed to achieve contact with these four people.

Table A.1 – *Response rates: depth interview survey*

	Number
Contacted by Business Debtline/STACS to take part in the research	403
Agreed to take part in the research	**53**
unusable responses	7
non-contacts	4
refusals	1
respondent died during fieldwork	1
Interviews achieved	**40**
no longer trading	27
still trading	13

Forty interviews were achieved with twenty seven people who were no longer trading and thirteen people who had experienced business problems but who were still trading at the time of the interviews. Twenty-three respondents were clients of STACS and seventeen were clients of Business Debtline.

Characteristics of the sample

Tables A.2 and A.3 give the demographic breakdown of the sample and some information about respondents' businesses.

Table A.2 – *Personal characteristics of the sample*

	Not trading		Trading	
Sex:				
Male	23		12	
Female	4		1	
	At time of interview	*When set up in business*	*At time of interview*	*When set up in business*
Age:				
29 or under	1	6	0	4
30–39	5	8	3	2
40–49	10	9	4	6
50–59	9	4	3	1
60 or over	2	0	3	0
Marital status:				
Married	21		12	
Divorced/separated	4		1	
Widowed	1		0	
Single	1		0	
Ethnic origin:				
White	24		9	
African Caribbean	1		0	
Indian/Asian	2		3	
Housing tenure:				
Owner-occupied	16		13	
Private rented	5		0	
Housing Association	2		0	
Local authority	1		0	
No home	2		0	
Economic status:				
Self-employment	2			
F/time employment	8			
P/time employment	4			
Unemployed	13			
Financial status:				
Bankrupt	13			
Not bankrupt	14			

Very few of the respondents were women and, of the women who did participate, only two were running businesses on their own. The rest had been/were involved in a business with their spouse/partner. They either appeared as the respondent because the inquiry to Business Debtline or STACS had been in their name or because they had subsequently split from their spouse partner. Respondents were of a wide age range with few obvious differences between those trading and not trading. The vast majority of the sample were married or in a permanent relationship. Few had dependent children living with them at the time of the interview but most had children who had left home.

The impact of business failure on housing status is clear. All respondents who were still trading were living in owner-occupied housing. Almost half of the respondents whose businesses had failed were living in rented housing at the time of interview. Virtually all these respondents had lost their owner-occupied homes when their business failed. Respondents with dependent children who had lost their homes after business failure were housed by Housing Associations or Local Authorities. Other respondents, who were not priorities for social rented housing, were forced to find housing in the private rented sector.

Two respondents had no homes at all at the time of interview. Both had given up their homes and lived on their businesses premises, one sleeping on the floor of a stock room. Neither had managed to find stable housing situations after their businesses had failed and both were staying temporarily with friends.

Table A.3 – *Respondents' businesses*

	Not trading	*Trading*
Nature of business:		
Retail	11	3
Service	14	7
Manufacturing	2	3
Time trading:		
Less than 2 years	4	0
2–5 years	12	3
6–10 years	8	6
11–14 years	0	1
15 years or more	3	3
Family involvement:		
Involved	17	4
Not involved	10	9
Trading premises:		
Traded from home	16	7
Separate premises	11	6

The importance of the first two years of trading in the success or failure of a small business is indicated by the respondents' in this study. None of the respondents who were still trading had been running their businesses for less than two years at the time of interview while four respondents who were not trading had closed their businesses during the first two years of self-employment. The vast majority of respondents' businesses closed sometime after the first two years but were still relatively new businesses at the time they failed. Respondents who were still trading had been running their businesses for longer than respondents who had ceased to trade – more than three quarters had been trading for six years or more at the time of interview.

More of the businesses which had closed had involved other members of respondents' families, conforming more to the 'family business' model. Trading from domestic premises was common among all respondents, most commonly as a way of reducing overheads.

THE INTERVIEWS

The interviews were conducted face-to-face by three depth interviewers who were experienced in working in sensitive areas and had worked with PSI in the past. The interviewers worked to a topic guide designed by PSI. The topic guide covered previous employment; reasons for becoming self-employed; reasons for business failure; experience of business failure; impact of business failure on respondent and their families; feelings about the future. The interviewers also collected detailed financial information on investment and financial arrangements at the start of self-employment and while the business was in operation.

The interviewers were fully briefed in July 1995 and fieldwork commenced immediately after the briefing. They also attended an interim de-briefing when half of the fieldwork was complete to discuss the direction of the research and assess the need for any further alterations to the topic guide. A final debriefing was held in September 1995.

All of the interviews were tape-recorded and fully transcribed. In addition, brief interview notes were written up by the interviewers immediately after the interviews. Despite concerns that respondents may have found the process of business problems or failure too difficult to talk about interviewers found that respondents were very frank and open. Moreover, the majority were exceedingly grateful for an opportunity to talk about their experiences. As a result, interviews were often long – up to two hours – and respondents were very honest about their feelings and perceptions of their situations.

A further concern – that respondents may find it too painful to relive their experiences – was also unfounded. Although one or two respondent were agitated or upset during the interview this was short-lived and interviewers were sensitive to the need to pause during interviews should this occur. In addition, interviewers were briefed to encourage respondents to contact Business Debtline or STACS for further counselling should they need to do so. This was never necessary and even respondents who were angry or upset during the interview generally found it a cathartic experience.

ANALYSIS

The interviews were analysed using qualitative analysis grids.

References

Barclays *Small Business Bulletin* Issue 2, 1997.

Berthoud, R. and Kempson, E. (1992) *Credit and Debt: The PSI Report.* Policy Studies Institute.

Birmingham Settlement Money Advice Centres and Research Unit (1991) *The Feasibility of Developing an Insolvency Advice Service in Birmingham.* Birmingham Settlement.

Blanchflower, D. and Oswald, A.J. (1996) *British Social Attitudes Survey 7th Report.* Gower Publishing Ltd.

Brown, J.C. (1994) *Escaping from Dependence – Part-time Workers and the Self-Employed: the role of social security.* Institute for Public Policy Research.

Campbell, M. and Daly, M. (1992) 'Self-Employment into the 1990s'. *Employment Gazette*, June, pp. 269–292.

Carter, C. and Cannon, T. (1988) 'Women in Business'. *Employment Gazette*, October, pp. 565–571.

Department of Trade and Industry (1994) *Small Firms in Britain in 1994.* HMSO.

Department of Trade and Industry (1997) *Business start-ups and closures: VAT registrations and deregistrations 1980–96.* Government Statistical Service.

Gray, C. (1992) 'Growth Orientation and the Small Firm'. In K. Caley et al, *Small Enterprise Development Policy and Practice in Action.* Paul Chapman.

Economic and Social Research Council (undated) *Small Business Research Programme.* ESRC.

Ford, J., Kempson, E. and Wilson, M. *Mortage Arrears and Possessions.* HMSO.

Hakim, C. (1989) 'New Recruits to Self-Employment in the 1980s'. *Employment Gazette*, June, pp. 286–297.

Johnson, P. (1986) *New Firms: An Economic Perspective.* Allen and Unwin.

Keeble, D., Walker, S. and Robson, M. (1993) *New Firm Foundation and Small Business Growth in the United Kingdom.* Employment Department.

Meager, N., Court, G. and Moralee, J. (1994) *Self-Employment and the Distribution of Income.* Institute for Manpower Studies.

Rowlingson, K. and Kempson, E. (1994) *Paying with Plastic.* Policy Studies Institute.

Storey, D.J. and Strange, A. (1992) *Entrepreneurship in Cleveland 1979–89.* Employment Department.

Storey, D., Watson, R. and Wynarczyk, P. (1989) *Fast growth small businesses: case studies of forty small firms in the North East.* Department of Employment.

Thwaites, A. and Wynarczyk, P. (1993) *Innovation and Financial Performance in Small Firms.* Centre for Urban and Regional Development Studies.